100 Things I Hate About Pregnancy

100 Things I Hate About Pregnancy

Kate Konopicky

Vermilion
LONDON

First published in the United Kingdom in 2005 by Vermilion, an imprint of Ebury Publishing Random House UK Ltd.
Random House
20 Vauxhall Bridge Road
London SW1V 2SA

Random House UK Limited Reg. No. 954009
www.randomhouse.co.uk

A CIP catalogue record is available for this book from the British Library.

ISBN: 9780091900120

Penguin Random House is committed to a sustainable future for our business, our readers and our planet. This book is made from Forest Stewardship Council® certified paper.

Printed and bound in Great Britain by Clays Ltd, St Ives plc

1. TESTING TIMES

You have your suspicions. Hopes, even, not to say fears. No point in putting it off any longer. It's best to know one way or another. Should you buy a kit or get a professional opinion? Whichever method you choose, it's going to be unavoidably toilet-based. You'd think in this day and age that you'd be able to tell if a woman was pregnant by a simple saliva swab, or maybe by just looking deep into her eyes. But no, at some stage wee is going to be involved.

So I trotted off to the doctor with a full bladder – it takes a day longer than something from the chemist but has the advantage of being free. Then I spent 24 hours twiddling my thumbs and trying not to think of what lay ahead. When the time came to make the phone call I hung about for at least an hour. No harm in putting it off for a bit longer. The answer to my question was going to be a little more important than the response to 'Have I got the job?', 'Did I pass the exam?' or 'Is that goal going to be allowed?' Whatever the doctor said might change my life forever, and I had to have my reaction ready. I practised phrases of joy and resignation before eventually dialling the number. The call itself was deeply disappointing. 'Yes, it's positive.' 'Oh, thank you.' Click.

Hang on, you've just given me the most important news of my life. Shouldn't we talk about this? I don't think my 'Oh, thank you' conveyed the right amount of elation tinged with anxiety. Perhaps I should ring back and explain. She sounded rather matter-of-fact and – if I'm honest – bored. Shouldn't there have been klaxons and bells? Game-show-type whooping and applause? Apparently not. I was forced to admit that the messenger couldn't give a toss whether I was pregnant or not. It wasn't to be the last time that my interesting condition proved to be of no interest whatsoever to other people. Damn.

2. HOW WAS I SUPPOSED TO KNOW I WAS PREGNANT?

You can't help it. Once the reality of pregnancy has sunk in, you start doing backward calculations. Was it that night of passion in a Runcorn motel? Had we started a baby because we were consumed with emotion, or because we had consumed too much cheap red wine? It would have been nice if conception had occurred under a starry Italian sky with the strains of Verdi in the background. Then we could have called the baby Firenze or Roma, instead of Basildon. But we foolishly neglected to leave the country before having sex, so we don't have any romantic stories to embarrass the child with in later years. Oh, hang on, I know when it must have been, because I remember the following week, having creosoted the fence and cleaned out the cat litter tray, I had that marvellous meal of steak tartare and unpasteurised cheese, washed down with about three pints of vodka. I had to take several paracetomol the next day. Oh *God*, what have I done?

Having just been presented with the greatest news of your life, for some reason your immediate reaction is not to tell anybody. So, while waiting for medical confirmation, the first scan, reassurance that I hadn't accidentally ingested a fizzing cocktail of baby-killing parasites I'd never even heard of before, I walked around with a gigantic sense of responsibility and nobody except my partner to share it with. The temptation to drop arch hints was sometimes overwhelming. And because nobody knows, nobody cares. Nobody treats you as anything special. People are all solicitude for great whales of women, but because you've only got a little cluster of cells and a flat(tish) stomach you're not part of the sisterhood yet. You are therefore fair game for elbowing commuters, unreasonable overtime demands and requests for help – usually with shifting heavy furniture, operating X-ray machines or removing asbestos.

Not wanting to look pathetic or give the game away, you try to behave as normal while bubbling over with untold tidings. It's just not fair. Plus the fact that while your closest family are still unaware of your condition, complete strangers might be privy to your secret.

The bloke in the chemist, for example, knows damn well why I have a prescription for folic acid tablets; the dental nurse needs to be told and even the woman in the bookshop is wondering whether I am buying *Baby and Childcare* for myself or a friend, but is, I trust, too polite to ask. It was just the first in a nine-month-long series of 'we'll just get this stage over with' phases.

4. SPREADING THE GOOD NEWS

Having kept it to yourself for a decent interval, you then have to announce your fecundity to friends and family before it becomes only too obvious to the general public. What should be a joyous outpouring of family togetherness is, of course, a minefield of potential argument as you realise that such important news has to be imparted in strict hierarchical order. Family before friends and all friends in quick succession so that nobody gets miffed because they were only the third to know.

I wish I'd been able to book a conference call. But I settled down with the receiver and started dialling. After a couple of embarrassing failures I decided that the direct way was the best. My father-in-law reacted to a rather coy 'You're going to be a grandfather' with a puzzled 'How come?' (If you don't know by now, the presence of your son needs some explaining.)

My side of the family wasn't much better. They had spent years replying to my chirpy 'I've got some news!' with a breathless 'You're pregnant!' only to be disappointed by me replying 'Er, no, I was going to say we've got a new fridge/the cat died/my rash has cleared up.' Bored with my barrenness, this time they refused to rise to the bait. No good pussyfooting around with 'Guess what!', only to get the suspicious reaction: 'You're not going to tell me about your rash again, are you?' The only way was short and to the point: 'Hello, I'm pregnant' – then I had to whip the receiver away to arm's length before mother/sister/best friend attempted to shatter it and my eardrum with a shrill whoop. Couldn't we have just hired a skywriter?

5. 20:20 HiNDSiGHT

When told my momentous news, someone inevitably claimed that they instinctively knew, just by looking deep into my eyes (or taking a discreet saliva swab, presumably). It was highly likely to be the same person who only days previously had not noticed my repeated refusals of the offers of double whiskies and Havana cigars, while planning joint holidays and remaining totally oblivious to my non-committal replies. While never actually being specific ('It was because your eyes changed colour'), they insisted they could tell there was something different about me, sometimes dating their instinctive knowledge to a time before I knew myself, or before I was even pregnant. I resisted the urge to snap 'Well, you could have bloody well told me, because I had no idea.'

6. 'BABY ON BOARD' BADGES PROMINENTLY DISPLAYED ON LAPELS

Not funny. Just twee.

7. A BODY OF EVIDENCE

I'd seen pregnant women before so I had a pretty good idea that at some point I would be lumbering around like a dinosaur with swollen ankles and varicose veins popping out at hourly intervals. An enlarged frontal area goes with the territory, but some of the other stuff came as rather a surprise. There's probably a very good reason why nobody tells you that being pregnant can cause your hair to come out in handfuls, your nails to split, your taste buds to shrivel, your gums to bleed and your skin to darken and go blotchy. As the hair fell out of my head it popped up in other places. The luxuriant line of dark fur that appeared between my belly button and pubis was particularly repellent, as was the nasty taste in my mouth, painful, heavily veined breasts and vaginal discharge. I felt that there was not one cell in my body that wasn't being affected in one way or another by this baby. I began to expect that when my earlobes went green or a second head started growing out of my armpit I would be told 'Oh, don't worry, it's just because you're pregnant.'

8. WAKE UP AND SMELL THE VOMIT

Wake up. Switch off alarm. Open eyes. Close eyes. Tentatively examine physical condition. Attempt slight movement. Stomach is immediately alerted and swings into action. Nausea, sweating and lavish vomiting follow. I feel sick, therefore it must be time to start my day. With watering eyes and a stinging throat. There must be an extra layer of enamel on the toilet by now, the one that's come off my teeth.

It's one of the cruelties of pregnancy that at the very time when you are scrupulously *not* doing anything the night before that might cause even the faintest of queasiness the following morning, you wake up feeling like a roistering, riotous reveller after a particularly debauched evening. Most people will tell you that morning sickness doesn't last very long. There's always someone, however, who knew a woman who was sick every single day for nine months. And they tell you all about it. Just when you're feeling too sick to attempt physical violence.

9. PLANNING (RATHER TOO FAR) AHEAD

There's a little lump of cells inside you about the size of a strawberry. You should be using your shrinking brain to calculate your vitamin intake, make shopping lists or fill out forms for maternity pay. Instead, your mind develops a previously unknown ability to plan ahead – up to about 40 years ahead in my case. It only takes about 20 minutes of serious mooning about (you can do it on the train while not getting a seat) to plan the strawberry's career, marriage and grandchildren. It doesn't matter that you might not even know if it's a boy strawberry or a girl strawberry; that just gives you an excuse for alternative daydreams. Whichever, it's definitely going to do something in the arts. It's definitely going to enjoy all the fame and success that was so cruelly denied yourself by a fickle world. Even if, by some gross miscalculation on the part of Mother Nature, it's not conventionally beautiful, it will have the self-confidence, intelligence, poise (and exquisite dress sense) that will make it instantly attractive to men, women, children and animals.

You start calculating how old you will be when it wins its first

Oscar, and wondering what you will wear for the ceremony. Dame Judi Dench still scrubs up pretty well, so you think you could probably make a decent entrance as long as you don't go mad and opt for something sleeveless. Or perhaps worldwide fame could get a little wearing. Maybe better to be an expert in a less obvious field, like the world's best lighting director. It could still get an Oscar for that, but without being pursued by the paparazzi (unless they wanted their flashbulbs fixed, perhaps).

The daydreams become more and more extravagant and rose-tinted and you just can't stop. It's lucky the poor little strawberry (presumably) knows nothing of your plans for its future – the ludicrousness of your ambitions would probably cause it to question its mother's sanity before it was even born. God knows in my case it would find out about my befuddled brain soon enough after it was born.

10. WETTING THE MOTHER'S HEAD

Swimming. Don't like it, never have, never will. I hate the smell, the noise, the plasters floating past your nose, the clothes dropped on the wet floor and the totally inadequate hair dryers. Put me on a hot sunny beach in a flattering one-piece and I'll think about it, but as far as I'm concerned swimming in a municipal pool is the nastiest form of water torture known to woman. But I felt I had to do it because it was good for me and so good for the baby, although it put me in such a foul temper it couldn't possibly have been good for the baby. Was this the start of a lifetime of self-sacrifice and tiresome chores? Yes.

11. READ ALL ABOUT IT

Once your pregnancy is common knowledge you are subjected to an onslaught of advice. And when people aren't helpfully passing on their foolproof methods for avoiding stretchmarks (boiling up your toenail clippings by the light of the full moon) or cures for morning sickness (just don't wake up in the morning) they are pressing on you their 'baby bibles'. All the books they couldn't possibly have given birth without. Believe me, there are quite a few – by no means all as good as this one. Admittedly, not ever having done this pregnancy thing, I thought an instruction manual might be helpful, so I mooched about in Waterstone's in a section I had never before entered.

While I was undoubtedly steeped in ignorance, the need for a few helpful hints was tempered by a vague feeling that I was supposed to know things instinctively. Women over the millennia have just done what comes naturally, without diagrams or professors of pregnancy telling them what to do, so having to resort to books seemed a bit of an admission of failure.

Still, forewarned is forearmed, so I chose a friendly-looking volume with lots of pictures in full, blooming colour, which over the months grew more dog-eared and more hated. It told me that at 12 weeks my baby could suck, swallow the liquid that surrounded it and pass urine. Yeuch. It also told me to give up smoking, eat lots of fruit and vegetables and not wear tight knee-length socks. Gee, thanks, that was worth £16.99 of my money. It was jam-packed with useful advice such as 'You may be a bit emotional and easily upset by little things' (which explains why I threw it across the room in a fit of temper, maybe). 'You will need bottle-feeding equipment (if you are going to bottle-feed).' I half expected it to continue: 'You will need breasts (if you are going to breast-feed).' The 255 pages of detailed information could have been cut down to a leaflet if it had not seen fit to tell me that I might be feeling tired yet be having trouble sleeping; that I should wear gloves for household chores if my nails were splitting; or that my clothes will be getting tight and I should look for attractive, comfortable clothes available from the standard selection in the shops. No, I shan't. I shall look for ugly, uncomfortable clothes that can only be found in an Armenian souk. And yet, with all the useless advice and pretty pictures, when I actually wanted to know something specific and quite important, the book remained strangely silent on the matter. I had to consult the doctor instead. When I mentioned that none of the books contained any mention of this particular symptom (see number 38) she said 'No, they wouldn't. Now go and buy yourself some comfortable and attractive clothes available from the standard selection in the shops.' No, she didn't say the last bit; she was actually quite helpful. Which is more than I can say for the bloody book.

12. HAVE YOU PUT ON WEIGHT?

Past the stage where your pregnancy is totally invisible (except, of course, to people who 'know' these things) and before your belly turns into a cartoon, there is that in-between stage when hideous mistakes can be made. I can't decide which is worse: being offered a seat on the train when I wasn't pregnant, or the suspicion that people assumed my belly contained not a baby, but the results of a diet of beer and chips. (Incidentally, it was only during pregnancy that my middle bit became a 'belly'. I've never referred to it that way before or since, but if it contains a baby your tummy, stomach, midriff or what used to be the region of your waist becomes, undoubtedly, a belly.) Trying to cover up a swelling with loose clothing just makes it worse. You really do look fat. Accentuating your bump with tight sweaters is an option – the sartorial equivalent of carrying a banner saying 'I'm not fat. I'm pregnant'.

Even so, some people still fail to get the message. They just keep on giving sidelong glances at your belly and you can see them thinking 'Is she or isn't she? Should I ask? Am I going to make the most awful faux pas? Better not mention it.' Which put me in a bit of a quandary. I had gone public up to a point, but how long should I put up with those quizzical looks before announcing to shop assistants and bus conductors that, yes, I knew what they were thinking and yes, I was pregnant? Because it was, frankly, none of their business. Why should I care if the woman at the deli counter thinks I was the one who ate all the pies? All I have to do is come back in a couple of months and all will become clear. But I did care, and found myself blurting out unnecessary information – just because I didn't want complete strangers to think I was a funny shape. What an idiot. It's bizarre what matters to you when you are pregnant.

13. WHAT MAKES pEOpLE THiNK THEY ARE FUNNY?

No, I don't want a piece of coal for my lunch and I haven't eaten the potting compost.

14. THE TERMS OF MY CONDITION

Every term to describe the state of pregnancy seems in some way unacceptable. 'In an interesting condition'; 'a mum-to-be'; 'in the family way'; 'preggers' – all unbearably coy and sick-making (as if you weren't feeling sick enough already). 'Up the duff'; 'in the pudding club'; 'up the spout'; 'knocked up' – vulgar and derogatory expressions to describe a woman with the future generation swimming about inside her. Minor royals are 'expecting a child', whey-faced stars of gritty 60s films get 'knocked up' – there is a stark difference. I certainly didn't think of myself as walking around with 'a bun in the oven', but short of responding to enquiries with a sentential 'Indeed, madam, I am quick with child' I would have to settle for 'pregnant' – despite the fact that even the bloody word sounds fat to me.

Even so, it wasn't as bad as the ghastly epithet I was landed with: 'elderly primogravidad'. Just because I was having a baby when I was over the age of 12. God knows that pregnancy and childbirth cause you to suffer all sorts of indignities, but being called 'elderly' really was the icing on the cake. I still haven't got over it, and I haven't got any younger, either.

15. Going spare in the spare room

Well, we've found a use for the spare room at last. I wouldn't describe it as the best argument for having a baby, but it certainly gives you a good reason for finally getting rid of dusty papers, old clothes and piles of unidentifiable things that might come in useful, but never have. The junk room is going to be a nursery. But how to decorate it?

Well, quickly, I thought, while I can still lift a paintbrush without fainting from the effort – and I'm not doing the ceiling. I'd witnessed this scene countless times in B-movies: for some reason there's always a slightly pregnant woman, dressed in dungarees and a spotless headscarf, slapping paint around a totally empty room and never getting any on the carpet. Perhaps an adorable little smear on her nose, for her husband to fondly kiss away when he gets home from work. My only consolation when watching these deeply irritating couples was that I knew damn well that they'd built the nursery on the site of an Indian burial ground or medieval torture chamber, and that soon enough paint on the carpet was going to be the least of their problems when the Witchfinder General turned up in place of the health visitor they had been expecting.

However, back in real life, the room still needed a bit of a wash and brush-up – and perhaps a few child-centred additions. The doomed couple are always toying with borders and murals and hanging up mobiles, but as I looked at our 'nursery' it occurred to me that I was going be spending quite a lot of time in this room and I was buggered if I was going to spend it staring glumly at bunny wabbits and teddy-weddys. No child of mine was going to be a prissy little wimp – I needed colour and vibrancy, a pleasant yet stimulating environment filled with objects of beauty and interest to engage the baby's senses. I also needed about two thousand quid to achieve all this, so a bit of a rethink was in order. Colour, we could do colour – as long as it wasn't weedy pastels. But not so bright with primaries that it would make me squint. Then I read somewhere that babies respond really well to black and white. Bridget Riley posters? I rejected that on the grounds that the nursery could end up as a migraine-inducing cell, which wasn't quite the effect I was aiming for. But while I was still aiming for an effect, time was passing. So we painted it white and put a cot in the corner.

16.   SCANTY SCANS

Now, I know people who take ultrasound scans do it for a living and have a pretty good idea of what they are talking about, but I really did suspect they were making it all up half the time. 'Look, there's the head and you can just see an arm there.' Frankly, all I could see was a smudge and a squiggle and a smudge. Deeply ashamed that I couldn't recognise my own child, even when shown a picture of it, I would agree blithely and try to memorise what the professionals had said, so I could disguise my ignorance to friends and family by repeating airily 'Look, there's the head and you can just see an arm there.' When one friend replied blankly 'Well, it doesn't look like anything to me,' I was hard put to explain what I didn't understand myself. But I think I got away with it. A mother has instincts for these things, you see.

17. THIS MIGHT BE A LITTLE COLD . . .

Belly gel. Not nice.

18. A 50-50 CHANCE

'Would you prefer a boy or a girl?' is way up there in the top 10 of boring, predictable questions that you really can't be bothered to answer. As the scan was not clear on the subject (ha! I told you it was just a smudge and a squiggle!), I didn't know the sex of my baby, so was scrupulously trying not to have any preferences in case I was disappointed. (I don't mean disappointed, of course, I mean surprised.) And it is a bit of a stupid question, if you come to think of it. Who is going to answer: 'Well, I would prefer a boy, so if it's a girl I shall just have to expose it on a hillside and try again'? So you end up replying to this inane query with a rather limp 'Well, we don't really mind as long as it's healthy' while inside you are shouting 'Ask me something interesting or go away!'

19. PLANNING PERMISSION DENIED

Birth plans were really not my strong point. When asked what my birth plan was I could only mutter vaguely 'Um, I plan to have a baby.' I had no clear idea about whether it should be born under water, in a bed or up a tree. How could I possibly know what was going to happen? I was also conscious of the experience of a friend of mine. Just as she was clearing her desk in readiness for a couple of weeks of rest and relaxation, her waters broke. You can imagine her reaction. It was not 'Oh joy! The miracle of birth is awarded to me even sooner than I had hoped!' It was more along the lines of 'Oh bugger! I haven't even sorted out a babysitter for its brother.' I don't know how she had planned her labour, but it certainly wasn't to have proud father *and* rather bemused first-born cluttering up the birthing suite. So I wasn't going to get caught out by making elaborate plans about musical accompaniment or travel arrangements for far-flung relatives, only to have them scuppered by an uncooperative baby who hadn't read my rules.

One firm conviction I did have, however, was that when the time came, I wouldn't care whether the sound system was belting out Brahms or Bachmann-Turner Overdrive. So, much to the disapproval of certain friends and professionals, who regarded this as a shameful lapse in forward thinking, I steadfastly refused to make any plans beyond getting to hospital in time for somebody else to sort it out. Pain relief? It depends how much it hurts. Who is going to be present? Some highly competent doctors and nurses, I trust. What am I going to wear? Not much from the waist down, presumably. And when it did come to it, I was proved right. When asked at 2am whether I would like my own midwife to be present I couldn't see much point in getting her out of bed as well, so answered (rather rudely, probably) 'You're qualified aren't you? You'll do.' In my defence, I have to say that I wasn't in a very good mood.

20. BUY, BUY, BABY

I felt a bit guilty when I first found out I was pregnant – just because I had recently bought an expensive winter coat. I would never have spent all that money if I'd known there was a baby on the way. Because of course now we were 'starting a family' most of my money was earmarked for far more important things than mere fashion items. After a couple of trips to Mothercare, however, I was jolly glad that I'd frittered away a couple of hundred quid on myself as I couldn't see it happening again for a few years at least.

Despite receiving a fairly respectable haul of cast-offs and presents, the list of things we had to buy was long and expensive. Even when it was still tiny, the baby would need something to sleep in and something to sleep on. It would need things to wear, lots of things to evacuate its bowels into, things to deal with the consequences of those evacuations, a thing to be washed in, a thing to be washed with, lots of things so it could be carried, driven and pushed around. All of it essential and quite a lot of it available only in an insipid shade of aqua that doesn't exist in the natural world – only in the minds of people who design baby equipment. (The baby never knew it, but the changing mat wasn't in fact plain white. It was face down so I wouldn't have to look at the horrible pattern in which small grinning animals featured largely. Considering their purpose, some changing mats have spectacularly inappropriate designs. Or is Winnie the Pooh supposed to be ironic?)

I wasn't practised at this sort of shopping. Show me a frock or a herbaceous perennial and I'm all efficiency and firm decision. Show me more than one type of steriliser and I have no way of telling their relative merits – it's not the sort of purchase you make on a monthly basis. Then, just when I thought I was pretty well set up, I'd be pootling around Boots, fingering breast pads and gloomily pondering the indignity of leakage, when I would notice something else on the shelves I hadn't even thought of. Do I need an insect net for the pram? I considered this for a moment before rejecting it with a contemptuous snort. Good grief, we're living in west London, not West Africa – this is the devious act of a cunning manufacturer manipulating my maternal instincts and capacity to worry over things that aren't going to happen. I dismissed insect nets from my mind and never thought about them again – until the baby was about three months old and sleeping peacefully in the garden when I saw the biggest horsefly in the world, possibly in the history of the world. Contemptuous snorts always come back to haunt me. (If you can be haunted by a snort.)

So, apart from insect nets and baby gyms, I dutifully shelled out for anything and everything I thought the baby would need. I didn't – couldn't – buy it all brand new, though. I made a little girl cry by handing over hard cash to her mother for the buggy she was far too big for, but which was apparently her most treasured possession and her best friend. The trauma of the expense of it all was bad enough, but I hadn't realised that shopping for baby would also involve the emotional trauma of a small child. It was a good buggy, though, after I had managed to wrest it from the sobbing girl's impassioned grasp.

21. GOD, THAT'S UGLY

Babies are everywhere. Throw a stick on any high street and you'll be bound to hit at least five. (That's a manner of speaking, by the way, and not to be attempted in earnest.) I'd never really noticed them before, let alone counted them, but being pregnant made me scrutinise every bundle with an interest bordering on the obsessive.

I obviously couldn't rely on the scan to give me any clues as to what this baby was going to look like, and there is – as yet – no test for ginger hair, so I had to let my imagination go into overdrive. No, really, I *had* to. The range of possibilities was endless – they didn't all look like Winston Churchill after all. Some of them were quite attractive. And some were not. Was mine going to be like that sparky little article with the cheeky toothless grin? Or was I to be saddled with a scowling slaphead with a murderous look in its eyes?

My extensive, if non-scientific, research taught me little except that very few white babies look good in yellow. They come in all shapes and sizes, apparently, so during any walk along a crowded thoroughfare I would idly pick and choose my favoured characteristics and try to ignore the ones I didn't much fancy the look of. 'I want that one's hair; that one's eyes; that one's hands and that one's rather fetching outfit.' Common sense might have told me that, given its parentage, I was highly unlikely to give birth to anything destined to be either tall or blond(e) but I couldn't stop peering into buggies and slings with feelings of envy or commiseration by turns. There was something of interest under every blanket, but the really scary ones were babies with what looked to me like unnaturally large heads. They made my eyes water just to look at them, and I would check the mother for signs of a John Wayne walk or permanent rictus of pain, before hurrying away with my fingers crossed. Why torture myself with things I couldn't do anything about? Because I was pregnant and therefore not responsible for my thought processes (see numbers 9, 12, 29, 32, 35, 37, 48 . . .).

22. JOINING THE PUDDING CLUB

Like babies, once you spot one pregnant woman you'll find them jumping out at you from all over the place. Except they don't jump very much, on the whole. Or skip or scamper or scuttle. They lumber into view with surprising regularity, and what do you do if you bump bumps? In the unnatural surroundings of the antenatal class you sort of expect to see a few other pregnant women and you all know what you're there for, but what is the correct procedure for chance encounters between pregnant women?

I'm not very good at striking up conversations with complete strangers, but two heavily pregnant women sharing a lift in complete silence seems like a snub to the sisterhood. Do you say anything? Bearing in mind that whatever you come out with is bound to be completely inane: 'Oh, you're pregnant as well.' 'Ah, just like me, then.' Do you give that strange little conspiratorial smile in recognition of your shared state, or do you just jump in with both feet and demand 'How sick were you then?'

I tried to avoid other pregnant women if I saw them by chance. I didn't like them and didn't want to share any secret smiles with

35

them. Pregnancy was my thing: nobody else in the history of the world had ever been pregnant nor would anybody in the future. I was incredibly special and couldn't bear anybody else muscling in on my experience. How could I be special if she was getting in on the act as well? How dare she copy me? Part of this dislike was probably engendered by the fact that I enjoyed swanning about being pregnant and pretending that nobody who wasn't pregnant could possibly know how I felt. Being confronted by somebody who did know how I felt and could probably call my bluff was more than I could stomach (or belly).

23. THE ANTENATAL CLASS STRUGGLE

One place where I was forced to admit that I wasn't the only pregnant woman in the world was, of course, the antenatal class. You have to go, don't you? They're only trying to help, after all, so the least you can do is show willing. But I wasn't the only one whose willingness was heavily disguised as embarrassed reluctance. Shuffling into an overly bright room dragging a father-to-be reeking of cigarette smoke was not my idea of fun but I was determined to make the most of it.

Bright-eyed and bushy-tailed, we all sat there nodding sagely as the brisk midwife tried to give us the benefit of her 20-odd years' experience of delivering babies. And very odd years they must have been. I wondered if she was as bored as I was. I tried to look as if I was memorising the stages of labour and girding my loins (literally) for some pretty rough treatment, but I was really doing what I always do when in a group of strangers: pricing clothes, guessing occupations and making outrageous and totally unfounded value judgements on other people's taste in partners.

I was forced to stir myself when it came to the practical side of our instruction, but frankly, lying on the floor pretending to have a baby just doesn't do it for me. And it comes nowhere near the real thing. We were also subjected to demonstrations with a hideous-looking plastic doll (not to scale, thank God, as it was about the size of a small pony) which, had it started life as a real baby, should rightly have been drawing its pension, and was about as far from looking like a bundle of joy as a rabid hedgehog. If there was any danger of me giving birth to something that looked like that I would have to reconsider the whole business.

Not the reaction our jolly instructor was hoping for, I fancy, but I admit I found the whole thing rather a chore. Which was nice, because that just made me feel guilty for not being enthusiastic. A mental burden to add to my physical one. Just what I needed.

24. I DIDN'T REALLY NEED TO KNOW THAT

There's stuff going on inside my body all the time that I don't feel the need to examine too closely. The digestive system, for example, starts with a lovely meal and that's as much as I want to know. What happens to my steak and strawberries after they have gone down my throat is a matter of supreme unconcern to me. However, when the eventual result of another natural act is not a bowel movement but a baby, it's a different matter. You're pregnant, so the world and his dog are suddenly falling over themselves to tell you exactly what will be happening inside your body at every moment – like you can do anything about it.

I did my best to avoid some of the more intimate details – it was enough to know that I was being drained of all available nutrients while my body was awash with hormones with no useful purpose except to cause the sort of startling mood swings that keep everyone on their toes, including complete strangers at bus stops. Helpful professionals would not allow me to wallow in my ignorance, however. I suppose they were right to point out that labour and birth shouldn't really come as a complete surprise, and I ought to know what was going to happen, but as with all professionals, sometimes I wish they'd get their terminology sorted out.

'Smear test' is a good example. If a ratcatcher can be called a rodent operative why can't a smear test be called something a little more fluffy and friendly? Like a wet wipe. But it was the mucous plug that nearly did for me. Before you have a baby you have to get shot of your mucous plug. I've got a mucous plug? Yes, the miracle of birth starts with the expulsion of a snot cork – and it doesn't come out of your nose. As it happens, I have no memory – thankfully – of this momentous event that heralded the start of a new life so I feel justified in saying that I *really* didn't need to know that. Had I been told that one of the first signs of labour is that your knickers might get a bit smeary I probably would have taken it in my stride, but *mucous plug*?

25. Old Wives and Their Tales

At least the professionals were technically correct in their pronouncements, if a little too graphic for my taste. The garbage that comes out of the addled brains of people who should know better sometimes beggars belief. Mucking about with a wedding ring and a bit of string is harmless enough – though also pointless as I didn't have an old wife on hand to tell me whether the ring is supposed to swing clockwise over your belly for a boy or vice versa. But having been told that breast-feeding is bad for you, eating too many carrots would give me a ginger baby, night air is bad air and so on and so on, I began to think there are still people out there who believe that if you are surprised by an octopus while pregnant you will give birth to an eight-legged baby.

You're not allowed to scoff, of course, because you are pregnant and therefore stupid, so you find yourself bombarded equally by the hard scientific facts and atavistic mumbo-jumbo about walking backwards through doors or always putting your right shoe on first – caught in the middle like a vessel for everybody else's opinion.

Such fun, nodding and smiling and promising on pain of death never to look at the new moon through glass, while inwardly screaming 'Shut up, you stupid old trout – your children are bonkers because *you* are, not because you didn't eat enough nettles!'

I know that women have been giving birth for millennia, but do you think, in the 21st century, we could lose the mumbling round the campfire stuff and actually be sensible about this? No? OK, fine, I promise I will never use scissors to cut my nails and be safe in the knowledge that my child will never grow up to be a thief. Or should that be cutpurse? Do you know what? I feel like snip, snip, snipping away at my fingernails and guaranteeing my child a free trip to Australia. Ha! What do you say about that, Mrs There-Are-More-Things-In-Heaven-And-Earth? Oh, you say that there are more things in heaven and earth than I could possibly understand and I'm pregnant and stupid and really shouldn't scoff and you know best. God give me strength.

26. ARE YOU SURE THERE'S ONLY ONE iN THERE?

Yes, I'm sure. I may be a bit scatty on account of my condition, but I did actually make a point of asking how many babies I was going to have. Call me old-fashioned, but I just felt I needed to know. So what are you saying? You think I'm unnaturally large? Or do you just think you're being funny? Well you're not.

27. Does my belly look big in this?

It's not so bad at first, of course, but as your waistline broadens and more and more clothes get shoved to the back of the wardrobe, ready for when you can fit into them again (don't hold your breath), your options narrow. I never realised how easy it was to pull on a pair of jeans in the morning until I couldn't. But you still have one choice left before it's too damn late to ignore your size: accentuate or disguise?

A few experiments with voluminous shirts were, frankly, disastrous. Plain ones just made me look like a tent; anything with stripes gave me the appearance of a dirty great marquee. I couldn't wear zipped trousers any more, but nice, comfortable, elasticated leggings were about as appealing as white stilettoes. Appealing or not, I was eventually forced to capitulate and spent months in a pair of stretchy maternity trousers. 'Maternity trousers'. Can you think of anything that sounds less attractive? Except perhaps 'maternity bra', 'maternity knickers' or 'pinafore dress'.

I read somewhere some advice to pregnant women: 'A pinafore

dress is smart and versatile.' ('Versatile' in this context means that you can wear it with or without a T-shirt underneath. Blimey, really pushing the fashion barriers – Vivienne Westwood look out.) This is quite wrong. A pinafore dress is one of the many things, like cat poo, to be strenuously avoided during pregnancy. It is an admission of failure in the fashion stakes and, paradoxically, very ageing, considering that you are dressed like a two-year-old. There's 'retro' and 'vintage' looks, and there's pinafore dresses. That's the look that says 'I'm pregnant and I've given up. All I need is a Peter Pan collar and a bed jacket to complete my fashion statement.'

As you might have gathered, I wasn't keen on smart and versatile pinafore dresses – which is saying something considering that I was actually grateful for the previously hated leggings. And if I didn't like 'pretty' clothes before I was pregnant, why on earth should I suddenly develop a liking for adorning my body with little floral patterns and discreet pastels? But what's a girl to do? You can wear a Carmen Miranda hat, Elton John glasses and hubcaps for earrings, but the most obvious thing about you is *still* going to be what you are carrying out in front.

I couldn't wait to get back into normal clothes again – or just different clothes, as the maternity trousers were beginning to look a little threadbare around the seams. Like some sort of fetishist, I had little fantasies about short skirts, basques and high heels; looked forward to squeezing into something really uncomfortable yet stunning; fingered rails of unsuitable clothes with longing, until I feared getting slung out of shops for acting suspiciously ('Is that a baby under your jumper or 500 quid's worth of shoplifted stock?'). At least I never sunk so low as to wear a pinafore dress.

28. THE NAME GAME

This is supposed to be the 'fun' part of pregnancy. In fact it is the part when you find out some frightening lapses of taste on the part of the baby's father. He, in turn, looks aghast at your various perfectly reasonable and attractive suggestions.

Family names could be useful, until you realise that all your favourite relatives have names like Gwladys, Hepzibah or Clarence. And it's not just the first names; a lapse of concentration and you could end up with a Kay Cole or Rose Bush, Richard Head or Benito Mussolini. If you're going for a middle name as well, do bear in mind that initials can spell things, and as soon as children can read, they will work out what those things are. I still remember the girl at school who had H.A.G. proudly stencilled on her schoolbag, and how hellish we made her schooldays. I know a Czech girl called Petra, which is a perfectly normal name, especially for Czechs. But she was brought up in England, and she suffered the same sort of treatment at school because everyone thought she was named after the Blue Peter dog.

Far from being fun, naming the baby is just another cause of potential trouble. After hours of sometimes heated discussion I eventually remarked gloomily 'Why don't we just call the baby "NO!" – it might save a lot of time in the long run.' Something nice, we wanted, not too outré, not too fashionable, nothing ridiculous or made up – how hard could it be?

And if you can settle amicably on something you both like, don't whatever you do tell anybody else. If anyone asks about names, just say you haven't decided, because whether you fancy Teresa or Trixibelle, Terry or Tarquin, somebody won't like it and won't hesitate in telling you so. I know, because to my eternal shame I did it to somebody once. A pregnant woman, remarking innocently that she quite liked the name Megan, was instantly showered with a barrage of abuse from her assembled 'friends'. 'Megan!' we all hooted, 'but your surname's Pugh! It would be like calling it Nerys Hughes! It'll come out dressed as a district nurse!' I don't think it was our influence, but the baby was a boy. Even so, I still feel guilty about daring to express an opinion on what parents should call their own children, but not everybody shares my sense of shame, so if you think you've decided on a name, keep it to yourself.

29.   HONEY, THE KID'S JUST SHRUNK MY BRAIN

I had another surprise when I was about four months 'gone'. (Gone where? Gone on the road to perdition? Gone to pot? Who makes up these things?) Those pesky, meddling scientists had been at it again, and come up with positive proof that women's brains shrink during pregnancy. And it was splashed all over the papers: everything is getting bigger except your mental faculties. Brilliant.

I remember the morning when the news broke. I had a meeting with an important client who was rumoured to be 'difficult'. It was my job to convince him, while trying to hide my belly under the table, that I was perfectly capable of taking on this complicated project. And all I could think of was 'He's seen the papers. He's seen my size and put two and two together. He knows I've got a full belly and an empty head. I can't say anything sensible.' I did get the job (probably because there was nobody else available to do it) and managed to complete it without any major cockups, but for the rest of my pregnancy I kept on expecting my head to rattle. Every time I forgot something, said something inane or couldn't remember why I had gone into the kitchen in the first place, I took it as a sign that in place of a brain the size of a planet I now had a small dried pea in control of my every function. It was small comfort that at the end of every news report there was a brief reassurance that it does grow back again. I have yet to see the evidence.

30. WHERE DOES THIS BIT GO?

Just when your brain is shrinking is when you are required to take a degree in engineering. When I say 'take a degree in engineering' what I mean, of course, is 'learn how to fold a buggy'. Same thing. Several hours of cursing and pinched fingers later I decided that it would probably be easier when I had my normal, slimline body back (forgetting that I would not be sprightly and unencumbered but hefting a baby as well). I promised to practise my technique for fear of folding my child in half or pitching it onto the pavement when my inexpertly assembled pram collapsed in a heap.

The car seat was no better. The instruction book was plastered with dire warnings about the seat being worse than useless if it wasn't fitted properly. I could understand the warnings, but the actual instructions were completely incomprehensible. Two of us were nearly in tears by the time we had wrestled the damn thing into place – and we still weren't sure whether we had fitted a safety device or a death trap. One strap in the wrong place and you might as well just park the baby on the roofrack for all the protection you will be giving it. I was hysterical and had to be slapped. So by the time I came to be fitted with a maternity bra my confidence was all shot to hell and I could only fumble hopelessly with straps and clips. How could anybody trust this idiot woman with a baby when she couldn't even cope with her own underwear? I thought babies were complicated enough, but nobody told me that all the equipment that goes with them is even worse. For a so-called natural process there seemed to be an awful lot of mechanics involved.

31. TRUST ME, I'M A DOCTOR

I knew I had to trust them, as they'd overseen the births of more babies than I had, but taking advice from a 50-plus man who'd never had a stretch mark, let alone a baby (although his belly was bigger than mine and he appeared to be developing a fine pair of breasts under his shirt) was sometimes a little hard to swallow. His brusque, 'pull yourself together, woman, I know better than you do and this is a perfectly natural process, although admittedly it might make your eyes water a little' attitude was faintly irritating, but in some ways I preferred it to the rather dippy 'this is the most beautiful experience in the world' approach of some of the soppier midwives.

I fail to see the beauty in varicose veins and vomit. (It's a bit like calling football 'the beautiful game'. What's beautiful about shouting and gobbing, I'd like to know?) One of these midwives really made me examine my maternal instincts when she stuck some sort of ear trumpet on my belly so I could hear the baby's heart beating and said 'There now, isn't that the most wonderful sound in the world?' I knew she meant well, but couldn't stop myself thinking 'Weeell, actually, given the choice between Mozart, birdsong and THDUNK

THDUNK I reckon there's no contest.' It was neither the time nor place, however, to start a heated discussion on the niceties of the English language, so I merely simpered dutifully 'Oh, yes, isn't it?'

32. THOSE MAGNIFICENT MEN IN THEIR MARKETING MACHINES

Why do people do this to us? Because they're in marketing and want to make a lot of money out of us. 'Do you want to give your baby the best possible start in life?' 'Well, if you put it like that, er, yes I suppose I do.' 'You can start before it is even born. Even in the womb the baby can hear, so play it our educational tapes (only £49.95) and it will pop out spouting Shakespeare.' Or some such persuasive rubbish. 'Oh really?' you scoff, certain that you can never be taken in by such a transparent ploy. And then, worming its way through your sensible carapace comes a scintilla of doubt. Maybe, just maybe . . . Am I denying my unborn child a glittering future in academia just because I'm too mean to spend 50 quid? Am I already not doing my job properly, failing in my responsibilities, destroying my child's chances in life? The marketing man's weasel words have done their job – your only hope is to grab yourself by the scruff of the neck, give yourself a good shake and shout 'Oh STOP IT! STOP IT!'

33. DON'T DRINK THE WATER AND DON'T BREATHE THE AIR

Raw eggs, soft cheese, cat poo, raw alcohol – I was well aware of the risks and knew what to avoid. Shall I tell you what else you should avoid at all costs? Headlines. Ones which scream at you that using a computer, or a phone, or an Etch-A-Sketch or a Swiss Army knife can all harm your unborn baby. What I thought of as fresh air is apparently a thick, bubbling soup of germs, fumes, spores and microscopic animals, all gagging to get up your orifices and into your womb.

Journalists talk dismissively about 'the latest health scare' as if it's not very scary – when it's absolutely terrifying. 'Should I be drinking tap water?' I asked myself anxiously. 'Should I switch to bottled mineral water or will I just find out in two months' time that the minerals concerned are in fact a deadly poison previously unknown to science? I suppose I have to breathe in occasionally but must remember not to do it if I'm anywhere near a new carpet, bonfire, paint pot or parrot.' Everything had suddenly become a potential health hazard. Benign everyday objects had turned into death traps and I was scared to open a newspaper, knowing that if the headlines didn't get me the germs lurking in the newsprint would.

34. WHAT DO YOU MEAN *YOU'RE* TiRED?

Oh, yes, he's had his fun. It's not him who has to put up with the consequences, is it? How dare he express weariness or complain that he has a slight backache? He has no idea what this is like. I'd better tell him. At great length. *Now* what's his problem?

35. LOOK OUT, iT'S GOT YOUR NOSE

It was a bit difficult trying to imagine what was going to come out at the end of it all. My collection of aches and pains, hormone rushes and mood swings was actually forming itself into a person. My imagination wasn't nearly vivid enough to paint a mental picture of a real human being so I tried to help it along a little by taking a long hard squint at the family this baby was going to be born into.

Bad idea. I was all right, of course, and it couldn't fail to become a wonderful individual if it took after me, but it wasn't a clone, unfortunately, and the rest of its gene pool was looking increasingly murky. What I had previously taken to be two perfectly normal families now seemed nothing more than a collection of big bums, short legs, premature bald spots, bizarre character traits – all with a powerful coating of mediocrity. Not an international reputation for anything among them.

I immediately ignored all evidence of kindness and intelligence genes and got myself all of a twitter about the size of its grandfather's nose. Ancient family photographs just looked like a parade of hatchet-faced miseries who never cracked a smile in their lives. Is it going to be a miniature version of one of us, or half-and-half, or revert back to take after that extremely sinister-looking woman in peasant's clothing whom its father claims is his great grandmother? I couldn't decide whether I was nurturing a human being to whom I was going to have a bond of unbearable closeness, or a complete stranger who would probably grow up wearing a smock and smoking a clay pipe.

I eventually understood the reality of being pregnant (after about eight-and-a-half months) but, despite all my wild imaginings and rose-tinted daydreams, could never really get my head around the fact that the result of all this was going to be a genuine person. With a huge nose.

36. WHEN CAN WE SEND IT OUT TO WORK?

Don't even think about how much this is going to cost. Beset by worries and anxieties, I could at least comfort myself with the thought that half the things I was worrying about would never happen. Those three-in-the-morning calculations, though, just wouldn't go away. This is going to cost. Big time.

In between wringing my hands in despair and rapidly filling out Lottery numbers, I could not make all the figures add up to something even remotely enough to keep us in nappies. There's always someone who will helpfully do the calculations for you, however, and every so often the papers will print the latest research on how much it costs to bring up a child. The figure always appears to be more than I have ever earned, or can ever hope to earn, in my entire life. It's billions. Even if we can keep our heads above water, suppose the boiler blows up, or the roof blows off, or I run out of shoes?

There's no way round it – your earning capacity isn't exactly improved much when you have a small baby, and that's precisely the time when you could do with some extra cash. Life is full of those little paradoxes, isn't it? In the end, I never found a solution, just a compromise. We agreed that I would lie around complaining about all my various physical discomforts, and it would be the baby's father's job to lie awake at night, sick with worry about our bank balance. I had enough to worry about just trying to keep my own balance.

37.   A CRYING SHAME

Yes, we all know how emotional you can be when you are pregnant. Apart from the towering rages at some imagined slight and completely unjustified panic attacks when you can't find a sock, there are the tears. Sniffling, sobbing and snivelling, blubbing, bawling and boohooing seem to represent the normal state of mind of a pregnant woman. And what a state it is. No wonder babies cry so much – it's a behaviour pattern they have learnt in the womb. They come out thinking it's normal to burst into tears every five minutes and not stop.

I have always enjoyed a good celluloid-induced weep, but can always pull myself together for the final credits. Not so when I was pregnant. I made the mistake of going to see a film in which a small boy sits in the bath and cries because his mother has gone away and his grandmother has just died and he's been dumped on a man who doesn't like children and doesn't speak his language. (It was *Kolya*, if you didn't recognise it from that description.) A large proportion of the audience was sniffing at this point, but one woman had large tears coursing uncontrollably down her cheeks which wouldn't dry even when the comic scenes cheered everyone else up. Guess who that was. Being fully aware that I was a complete embarrassment to my companion didn't help much either, and every time he irritably passed me another tissue it just made me bawl even more. By the end of the film (which has a happy ending, luckily, otherwise I would have been led away to a padded room) I was swollen-eyed and blotchy, with a blocked nose and a serious mascara problem. I looked as if I'd spent the last hour or so in a boxing ring rather than watching a feel-good movie. I can watch it now with no emotion whatsoever – except cringing humiliation at the memory of my pathetic performance.

38.   Ow!

Browsing happily in Hatchards in Piccadilly Circus one day, I was suddenly struck by a fierce pain in my side. This time, the panic was real and justified. I had no idea what was going on and my only thought was to get home, like a wounded animal. Sudden, severe pain was not covered until you got to the labour stage, and it was far too early for that.

A period of intense anxiety followed until I could get to a doctor. What she told me made me incredibly relieved – then rather cross. It's not uncommon, apparently, so why had nobody told me this could happen? The baby had snuggled itself down into a comfortable position lying with all its weight on a large nerve. Nice. 'It will only hurt if you stand or walk for long periods,' the doctor told me. A 'long period' turned out to be about 10 minutes, as it happened. I considered how a shooting stick might cope with my increasing bulk, as for the rest of my pregnancy I couldn't even get to the high street without sitting down at regular intervals. The washing up had to be done in shifts and popping out to post a letter took about a week. 'I feel fine,' I would say, 'apart from having to behave like an 85-year-old invalid, everything is just dandy.' The baby was obviously perfectly happy, so even though I could feel it doing somersaults, it never actually shifted far enough to stop pressing down on that same nerve. Not physically possible, you would have thought, but there's a lot of stuff about pregnancy that appears to be physically impossible.

39.   NOT IN FRONT OF THE CHILDREN

It can hear everything, you know. Now why is that so spooky? Because you're never quite sure whether it also understands and remembers. Should I be watching scary movies in case it comes out howling like a werewolf? (I'll give *Alien* a miss, that's for certain.) Should I be giving it little tips on childbirth ('For God's sake, point your toes, keep your arms close to your sides and don't start yelling until you can see the whites of the midwife's eyes'), or telling it amusing little anecdotes so it doesn't get bored in there and start picking at the wall coverings?

Once, when a door slammed, I jumped, the baby lurched and we both nearly ended up on the floor, so I knew that it was well aware of outside noises. I could feel it doing the hand jive when music was played and butterfly stroke whenever the theme tune to *The Archers* came on the radio. And if I had no idea what type of little personality was forming in there, was it getting a pretty good idea of what its mother was like just by listening to what I was saying? Especially as a lot of what I was saying was decidedly not for youthful ears. I noticed the baby was very quiet when I was shouting a stream of choice obscenities – obviously shocked to its core by my coarseness and vulgarity, but not really in a position to walk away. I felt obliged to apologise profusely: 'Sorry, baby, don't listen to me. I was just a bit cross – I'll explain about politicians when you're older. Try not to make those your first words.'

Naturally I talked to my baby (well, a bit unnaturally, actually, as I felt a little self-conscious addressing remarks to my belly button) so that it would recognise my soothing, loving voice when it was born. Although, presumably, my voice would only sound the same if I held the baby's head underwater and bellowed into an echo chamber – but perhaps it would recognise my vocabulary. On the whole, I hoped that the baby was no more than vaguely acoustically aware. The idea of being permanently eavesdropped upon just made me realise how much of my singing was tuneless and how much of my talking was rubbish.

40. I'VE NEVER LIKED BLOOMERS

Just because I'm pregnant you needn't expect me to be radiant. People feel they ought to tell you that you look blooming, when you both know what they really mean is blooming awful. A pregnant woman who isn't walking around in a sort of luminous glow is a huge disappointment to everybody else – just as everyone expects a bride to be 'beautiful', even if she's got a temperature of 103, a raging hangover or two heads. Pregnant women with puffy eyes and dull hair are really letting the side down – aren't you supposed to be at the pinnacle of your beauteous womanly charms, dearie? I think this is a cruel myth put about by people who don't care to know the reality of hair loss and eczema.

I have a theory that all pregnancy does is emphasise what you've already got, so that naturally fresh-faced women still look naturally fresh-faced, *even* when pregnant. The rest of us, with a tendency to slightly greasy hair or the odd spot, end up looking like a pizza floating on an oil slick. So that's nice. Just when I'm not exactly looking my best, I'm subjected to slightly puzzled scrutiny from people who can't understand why I'm not looking so much better. Why am I not visibly suffused with health and vitality? It's because I'm pregnant, stupid.

41. SHOULDN'T YOU BE PUTTING YOUR FEET UP?

Fortunately or unfortunately, the days are gone when you had to spend your entire pregnancy in a sort of purdah, regularly having fits of the vapours and your temples dabbed with eau de Cologne. It sounds quite appealing, actually, but admittedly not entirely necessary. We have been found out: we're not ill, we're just pregnant, and unless you are very unlucky a normal pregancy will contain days when you feel positively chipper. Those days full of energy and bounce are there to make up for all the other days when you feel like a wet dishcloth only fatter, and should be embraced with relief and glee. Which is why it is so annoying, when you are merrily attacking the kitchen cupboards with a welcome burst of vigour and vim, to be told that you should really be lying down in a darkened room. No, I am not overdoing it. Do you think I'm stupid? I know what I feel like and if I start feeling tired I will have a rest. Why must people interfere so much?

42. PUT YOUR BACK INTO IT, WOMAN

The kitchen cupboards may be sparkling clean but today I couldn't lift a Brillo pad if my life depended on it. I am weary, washed-out and whacked. Go away and let me lie down in a darkened room. This is the very day, of course, when all the overly concerned biddies hovering around with eau de Cologne wet wipes are replaced by herds of booming hockey players telling me there's no point in lying about like a droopy drawers because it's going to get a lot worse, you know. The very fact that I am at the pitch of exhaustion and want to weep bitter tears of self-pity is the cue for some helpful old battle-axe to tell me that she was shovelling coal when her waters broke and she didn't stop until she'd filled the bunker.

You know what? I don't much care that you gave birth to triplets while juggling flaming hamsters and running the rail industry at the same time. I feel like shit, I am entitled to feel like shit and nobody, least of all some self-congratulatory dimwit with a short memory, is going to make me feel guilty about it. Why must people interfere so much?

43. YOU'RE NOT ILL, YOU'RE JUST PREGNANT

Oh, but you do feel guilty. Suddenly the world seems to be full of pregnant women bouncing around like two-year-olds, flaunting their vigorous good health in your wan and tearful face. At times like these, feeling feeble is an admission of failure, and you get the distinct impression that if other women can dig the garden, erect buildings and run small countries while heavily pregnant, then people are assuming that your inability to get off the sofa must be a sham. You might whimper 'No, honestly, everybody is different and I was all right last week, I'm just feeling a bit low,' but you're obviously just not very good at being pregnant, and you should follow the example of other (better) women.

Guilt is just what you need right now in your enfeebled state. Unlikely to be able to shake it off with a toss of your head (because you have a headache) and a bright laugh (because you are never going to laugh again as long as you live), the guilt will settle over you like a blanket of gloom and all you can do is wail weakly 'Why me? Why do I feel so rotten? Why is my head glued to the pillow when I should be changing the bed and running a small country?'

Pregnant women who feel fantastic all the time (aberrations of nature, I know, but apparently they do exist) shouldn't be allowed out. They just give a bad impression, and make non-pregnant people (men and, more specifically, the baby's father) think there's really nothing to this pregnancy lark and you shouldn't be making such a fuss. Which is simply not fair.

44. NO, REALLY, YOU SHOULDN'T HAVE

You know why the Americans call it a baby shower? Because you get showered with useful and attractive gifts for yourself and your baby. All bright and shiny and new and wrapped in pretty paper and ribbons. Apparently we have a different system over here. True, I had my share of useful and attractive gifts, but I also had quite a large share of things that Oxfam would have had no hesitation in incinerating. Sorting through a bin bag full of stained vests was not my idea of a baby gift bounty. And the toys! 'Oh, you must have these, my boys loved them' actually means 'Now my boys have grown out of and totally wrecked this pile of plastic junk I'm going to off-load it on to you because I can't be arsed to do anything else with it and it's cluttering up the cupboard under the stairs.'

A pregnant woman is like a beacon for people with things to get rid of. As if you haven't got enough to do without disposing of other people's rubbish. And it's not like you're allowed to select what you want; you have to appear grateful for everything that gets dumped on you. So when the baby books tell you that you may have a burst of energy and feel like cleaning the house from top to bottom, what they are trying to say is that you'd better have a jolly good clear-out, otherwise you won't be able to get through the door without tripping over slightly broken dumper trucks and incomplete sets of chocolate-smeared Lego.

50. WE KNOW WHAT YOU DID LAST SUMMER

When I was big enough to be obviously pregnant and not just fat or badly dressed (or should that be *as well as* fat and badly dressed) I began to dread going out in public with my partner. The father of my child and the love of my life was now a source of acute embarrassment to me. It was nothing he had done; it was just that I knew that everyone who saw us together was imagining us having sex.

It was not a pleasant thought to have all these complete strangers thrusting their lurid imaginings into my head. I felt like accosting passers-by and saying 'It's not what you think – he's my brother', at the risk of them having even more lurid imaginings. How did I know they were doing it? Because I was doing exactly the same thing with every couple I saw shopping in Mothercare or supporting each other through antenatal classes. Once these thoughts have popped into your head it takes something pretty dramatic to pop them out again, and I was constantly having to banish some rather unpleasant mental images from my mind. If pregnancy didn't make me nauseous, the thought of her and him 'trying for a baby' would be guaranteed to make me a little queasy.

51. THE CHAMBER OF HORRORS

Part of my antenatal course was a guided tour around the birthing suite. Why? Just to put the fear of God into me, I suppose. If it was supposed to be reassuring, it wasn't. But it was a great spur to an overactive imagination. Other people may have seen a clean, largish room with a bed and lots of gleaming, efficient-looking equipment. I saw a soulless, intimidating space crammed with instruments of torture – and that included the perfectly harmless bed. Not very nice things were going to happen to me in this place. Calling it a 'suite', as if it was a rather high-class hotel room, didn't fool me one bit. They could at least have put some pictures on the walls – a few throws and scatter cushions would have brightened it up no end and made it look much more friendly. But the hospital had gone for the brisk efficiency look, and the effect was one of municipal menace.

Not to mention some really ill-advised decorating decisions. My baby was going to be born in a room with an olive green dado rail and pale blue blankets. Oh dear, oh dear. I'd better get it out of this place as soon as possible before it got the impression that the world was made of faded blue ticking and cracked brown lino. Hadn't these people ever heard of Ikea? And didn't they know that the proper place for stainless steel is the kitchen?

52.   OF COURSE, IT WAS 37 HOURS WITH MY JACK

Mention that you are going to the dentist and it's a cue for everyone present to launch into their gory molar stories. Nobody has ever suffered as much as them under the dentist's drill or had such pain inflicted in the name of good health. You'll never hear anyone saying 'Oh, the last time I went to the dentist I had a couple of fillings and it was fine.' It's the same with pregnancy.

The number of women who tell somebody with labour looming 'Yes, he came out like a rat down a drainpipe – I barely had time for gas and air before he popped out' are far outnumbered by those anxious – even eager – to relate their lurid tales of three-week labours, severe complications, unsympathetic doctors and unbearable pain.

Why do they do that? We all know that having a baby is likely to smart a bit, and we all know that you're supposed to forget about it once it's over, not inflict blow-by-blow accounts of your misery on somebody who hasn't yet been through it and might perhaps be a little apprehensive. And length of labour is not, I repeat *not*, a competition. Being in labour for three hours longer than the next woman does not make you a better person, just better at counting. After all, how do you really add up the length of a labour? If you start with the first twinge, then you could claim to have been in labour for 18 hours, even though for the first 15 you may have suffered no more than mild discomfort and severe boredom. No, 18 hours of labour makes you sound brave and stoical, as if you have been constantly thrashing about on a bed of unalleviated pain and should be congratulated for it. I can't think why, and I can't think why people feel the need to bombard pregnant women with unnecessarily scary stories about the hellishness of labour. And the same goes for your bloody wisdom teeth.

53. DO YOU HAVE ANYTHING WITHOUT STORKS OR TEDDIES?

I know that babies are sweet, innocent little things, and nobody in their right mind would want to dress them in camouflage outfits or give them teddies with attitude, but why do all their accessories have to be in such toe-curlingly poor taste? Never before had I been bombarded with such an avalanche of bunnies, hedgehogs (hedgehogs? a strange choice for a cuddly animal) and baby bears. Everything from stationery to bed linen to nappy buckets was decorated with hords of skipping sea lions or lambs or non-gender-specific babies with blond curls. And it was all so pale – I might have been screaming out for something in burnt orange or Air Force blue, but apparently babies can't cope with anything darker than an insipid pink, and would be permanently traumatised by a bib or high chair without an animal motif.

To think that people have gone to a great deal of trouble to draw and design these things, just in order to annoy me, so it seemed. And I imagined that after the first couple of years of the baby's life, I would have to spend the next two years explaining that no, we can't have a lion as a pet because, despite what it might look like on your cereal bowl, a lion's *breath* would probably kill you, let alone its teeth and claws. And I know the lamb looks sweet, but do you realise what you had for dinner last night? I'll give you a clue, sweetheart – it wasn't a lion and it wasn't a hedgehog.

Why was Jackson Pollock never approached to design baby accessories? Colour, spontaneity and a good deal of mess – perfect! Oh, I forgot, babies can do that perfectly well for themselves. With the addition of smell.

54. MODEL PREGNANCIES

Why do pregnant women in photographs always look so irritatingly wholesome? I swear the models are chosen to look as if they've never worn lipstick or nail varnish, let alone smeared lipstick and chipped nail varnish. Their glowing faces and tidy hairstyles beam out from the pages of mother and baby books like beacons of purity. These women have never even been kissed, much less done the beast with two backs.

I imagined them having their babies in a controlled, discreet fashion involving a little hot water, linen sheets, lacy nightgowns and perhaps a couple of quiet gasps as the baby slips out, already washed, into its beribboned christening gown. Not for them the blood and loud swearing of a normal birth.

They may possibly have had their tattoos and piercings airbrushed out, but somehow, from their self-satisfied looks, I doubted it. And I know, I just *knew*, that when they became mothers they would never shout at their kids or forget to iron their school shirts. Of course no editor would ever put a photo of a normal pregnant woman into a book, but do we really have to suffer such a loathsome parade of perfection?

55. PUTTING MY WORST FOOT FORWARD

Identifying strongly with Imelda Marcos was something I never thought I would do, but it took a bout of pregnancy to make me realise that her obsession with footwear may have had a point. A woman needs shoes. All those little high-heeled numbers mouldering away in the back of the wardrobe were crying out to me, resentful at being cast aside like old boots when they were the pinnacle of foot fashion and deserved to be worn.

Not a chance. Not only was I getting fatter, I was getting shorter as well as my heels lowered and finally disappeared altogether to be replaced by sensible flats with broad toes. I was wearing sensible shoes! How could this have happened to me? I hadn't been planning on abandoning my heels until they started interfering with my Zimmer frame, but here I was, half expecting to catch myself deliberating the relative merits of tartan versus velour carpet slippers.

It was a mental pain I had to endure to avoid a physical one. With my centre of gravity shifted, an aching back, swollen ankles and feet like globe artichokes, any heels higher than half a centimetre would have put me at risk of varicose veins at best and at worst a broken neck. So I padded around at my normal height (not very tall) and wondered whether I would ever again be able to produce that pleasing sound of clicking heels on parquet. Would my twinkle-toed gait have been permanently changed to a down-at-heel shuffle?

When I wasn't being Imelda Marcos I was identifying with Jack Lemmon in *Some Like it Hot*, watching Marilyn Monroe skipping daintily down a station platform in shoes that Imelda would have killed for. 'How do they do that?' he asks with evident awe. How? They don't get pregnant, that's how.

56. Damn, I've just washed THAT

I know how to handle a knife and fork – I've had a lot of practice. Under normal circumstances I think I can get through a meal without throwing food around, filling my lap with soup or covering the floor with stuff for the dog to clear up. I have been known to drink a full pint of liquid refreshment without spilling a drop. So why is a large belly such a magnet for food – I mean on the outside? Not just crumbs, which can be discreetly brushed away, but anything likely to stain, stick or smell will attach itself to your front while you're not looking – even when you are looking these marks appear magically like stigmata. I couldn't get up from the table without at least one large oily patch displayed prominently on my belly (it was olive oil, not chip fat, honest).

It really adds to your air of graceful elegance to have food stains all over your clothes, really makes you look like a competent and confident human being. Which is to say, it makes you look like an unsavoury slob incapable of getting food into her mouth with a normal success rate. I took to draping my protuberance with tea cloths before attempting any food consumption, and totally gave up on beetroot salad and chicken tikka masala. I pondered the advantages of a full body-bib over just eating naked with a bucket and sponge to hand. I decided that going down the bucket and sponge route probably wouldn't be acceptable in restaurants, and a full body-bib wouldn't do much for my image, either. 'Oh well,' I thought, dabbing hopelessly at a silk shirt (which is now a silk duster), 'it's all good practice for weaning.'

57. BELLY DANCING

Being kicked out of bed by something that hasn't even been born yet serves as a timely reminder of what your life is going to be like for the foreseeable future. Whether it be from a kick or a yell, get used to the idea that your sleep is no longer your own and is going to be violently interrupted at regular intervals by the amusing antics of your child.

The baby's first movements are a cause for great excitement. If you're lucky you can get some sort of communication going with a system of knocks and kicks ('Kick once for "yes", twice for "I don't understand you, I haven't acquired any language yet"'). After a while, friends demanding to see your belly ripple and insisting on putting their ears against your midriff can get a little tiresome. Nobody asked to feel my muscles when I wasn't pregnant, so I'd be obliged if you would refrain from pawing me now. And, baby, two o'clock in the morning is not the time to start disco dancing. (Well, actually, it is, but you're not supposed to know that for a good few years yet.)

58. SORRY, I THOUGHT I WAS NORMAL FOR A MOMENT

It may be difficult to believe, but you can actually forget about your condition for a few seconds at a time, and you don't have to be in a deep sleep or hypnotic trance. This usually means that you do things like miscalculate your girth and bump into things, absent-mindedly reach for a vodka and tonic or sink into a low armchair and find yourself unable to get up again. And I'll never forget the collective gasp of horror from a group of friends who saw me jump off a (very) low wall when I was six months pregnant. Sorry, I just forgot! I'm not sure whether they were horrified at my carelessness with my precious load or if they were concerned that I might cause something unfortunate to happen and they would have to do something about it. Either way, they made me feel terribly guilty and I had to promise to be more careful in future. Forgetting I was pregnant was another thing I wouldn't have thought physically possible until I did it myself.

59. Oi, MUM!

If you do occasionally wander off the point of your existence and think about something other than being pregnant, there's nothing like being forcibly reminded by a sharp kick in the ribs. This usually causes you to curse loudly in the middle of a sensible conversation or, even worse, in the middle of the quiet bit in a service of remembrance. Believe me, it's not funny when it happens to you.

60. LABOURING BEFORE LABOUR

Of course, as a modern, go-ahead type of girl, you foolishly maintain that you will continue to work for as long as possible into your pregnancy. Everybody expects you to, anyway, and would take a rather dim view of somebody who downed tools at the first signs of swelling. This is fine when the baby is barely making its presence felt and you're feeling fecund but not yet rotund. As time passes, however, your leaving date seems to be remarkably close to your due date. Actually, a couple of months off before the baby arrives sounds like a mighty fine idea and you wonder why you didn't think of it before.

Everybody is outwardly concerned about a pregnant woman, insisting you should go home early if you feel tired and not work too hard. Behind your back you suspect they are saying that you are not pulling your (considerable) weight and there's not much point in you being there anyway if you can't do the work. Grappling with a mixture of guilt and resentment, not to mention the daily grind of travel to work, is no way to spend the final months of pregnancy, but chucking it in looks like wimpishness. And you don't get paid. Although, considering you can get compensation for a broken finger, there should be some hefty monetary recompense for all the rigours your body is being put through. Until that day (expect hell to freeze over at roughly the same time), we continue to pretend that working is exactly what we want to do for as long as possible, and the idea of lying on the sofa with a trashy novel couldn't be further from our minds.

If you want to keep up the pretence, when a colleague informs you briskly that there is a bit of a problem with the Popkiss account, it's best not to wail peevishly 'But I'm *pregnant*!' No matter how much you might want to. Oh yes, everyone is terribly solicitous when they don't need you to do anything, but when you are required to stir your stumps, pull your finger out and generally faff about a bit, it's 'Baby, schmaby, woman, get your arse into gear'. All you can do is faint, vomit or – best of all – go into premature labour (or pretend to). That'll teach them to ignore your physical condition – or your mental attitude.

61.   WHY, I MUST BE IN LILLIPUT

It's not just your brain that shrinks when you are pregnant. It goes without saying that what you thought was a perfectly normal wardrobe has been transformed into something that consists almost entirely of tiny child-sized clothes that you can't ever imagine having fitted into. Doorways get narrower, low tables now appear to be about three inches off the floor and impossible to reach, and as for chairs, well, what happens to them is just spooky. I expected my clothes to get tight, but not my furniture. I avoided chairs with arms for fear of getting stuck and having to walk around with one permanently fixed to my bum, not knowing whether to call the paramedics or the fire brigade. Or a carpenter.

The kitchen was never big, but now it was miniscule and full of obstacles to bash against. My own house was conspiring against me to make me feel like an elephant in a Wendy house – a barn might have been a more comfortable living space. Until I and all the stuff around me returned to normal size I was forced to recalculate all movements – a bit like trying to park a bus after having driven a Mini all my life.

It made life a little challenging, but I realised why the frontal bulge is so often referred to as a 'bump'. It could equally well be called a bash, collide, thud, bang or wallop.

62.   IS THERE A LOO WITHIN WADDLING DISTANCE?

Bladder control – or, more accurately, the lack of it – hadn't really bothered me much since I was about two years old. I didn't know my pelvis had a floor until I discovered a flaw in it. Surely incontinence is an affliction of the very young and the very old, not someone who is supposed to be in the prime of her life and bursting with good health? (Don't mention bursting again, please.)

I hadn't been looking forward to nappies much, but gradually came to appreciate their convenience when I couldn't find a convenience. Neither had I noticed the complete dearth of public toilets in useful places, and had to plan shopping trips and short journeys to the bottom of the road with routes that would accommodate my complaining bladder.

Running taps, fountains and babbling brooks had to be avoided at all costs, and any building I entered had to be reconnoitred immediately for toilets. There wouldn't be any time to start wandering around looking for the Ladies when that old familiar feeling came upon me. No point in snapping at me 'Well, you should have gone before we came out!' because I had. About 17 times. There was only one word for it (well, two, actually): bloody inconvenient.

63. YOU'VE MADE YOUR BED

Admittedly I made the decision to have a baby, so I would have to put up with any attendant inconveniences. Most people do make allowances for pregnant women and don't make them do cartwheels or carry heavy loads (or another heavy load). There are some, however, who seem to resent their presence to the extent of actually going out of their way to make things difficult. 'Don't expect any concessions from me,' seems to be their attitude, and they can get really quite aggressive about it. Especially when it comes to seating arrangements.

Getting a seat on a London tube train can be a matter of some triumph, I know. When I do manage it and then see a pregnant woman get on I think 'Oh, bugger, now I'll have to get up again.' But I do it with good grace because I know her need is greater. I notice, however, that other commuters aren't exactly forming an orderly queue to give up their seats to a woman in a state of some largeness. (You can sometimes confuse these people into getting up for you by being pregnant *and* carrying a walking stick.)

Pregnant women are now sometimes forced to *ask* if someone in

107

a carriage full of people will get off their arse and let the future generation have a little rest, but I could never manage that level of assertiveness, especially when I was feeling sorry for myself.

I remember standing in front of one man who knew damn well I was there, ankles swelling visibly. I knew he knew because of the way he defiantly snapped his newspaper and wriggled his bum more comfortably into his seat. Although he didn't say anything, every atom of his being was yelling at me 'It's not my fault you're pregnant' (well, certainly not, I would never have such an ill-mannered boor as father of my child). 'You've made your bed, now you can lie on it.' Every atom of my being was yelling back 'I don't want to lie on a bed, but a seat would be nice,' but obviously not loudly enough because he never got up. He left it to a woman further down the carriage, whom he probably despised as much as he did me. I hope that man suffers from piles.

64.   I AM YOUR WORST NIGHTMARE

Far outnumbering those who resent us are people for whom a pregnant woman is an object of fear. In an advanced state of pregnancy I had occasion to go into an office to finish off work I'd done at home. I waddled into a room full of 20-something singletons and parked my bloated body behind a desk. It was about two or three weeks before my due date and I felt fine, but they weren't to know that. To them, I was obviously about to blow.

When, in my usual fashion, I started barking and growling at the computer screen they all jumped up and started piping shrilly 'Are you all right?', obviously expecting nasty things with blood and screaming to start happening. 'I'm fine, it's just playing silly buggers with the headings,' I remarked mildly, to general relief, and returned to my work. I continued to snarl and swear at regular intervals, got the job done and waddled out again like a ship in full sail, leaving behind me a bunch of pale-faced nervous wrecks. Honestly, what did they think I was going to do? Obviously they had all been watching too many TV dramas about babies being born in bus shelters, up mountains or behind filing cabinets. I'd never thought of myself as an alarming person. A figure of fun, maybe, but never a figure of fear. I may be big, but I'm not scary.

65. WHEN'S iT DUE?

Another tedious question you have to answer a million times. Once, only once, in all that time was I able to answer truthfully 'It's today.' Unfortunately, I was talking to an ambulance driver at the time (long story) so instead of leaping away in horror, he simply grinned broadly and offered me a lift in the back if I needed it. Funny man.

66. ENJOY!

Trying to cram in as much social life as possible before it disappears completely is not always a good idea. A quiet meal in a restaurant seemed like a welcome break until I convinced myself that people were nudging each other, pointing and tutting when I had a glass of wine, which rather ruined the enjoyment. Pubs are smoky, and the idea of nursing a glass of orange juice in an establishment that is there for the express purpose of consuming alcohol is an affront to genuine pub-goers.

Parties are even worse. If you go to a party you are not supposed to feel tired and want to sit down all the time. That's not really the point. And even if the jollities start off all right, there is nothing more dispiriting than watching other people get drunk – I thought I missed alcohol until I saw the effects it could achieve over the length of an evening.

One friend made the massive error of being pregnant during the Millennium celebrations. 'Oh, what fun that was,' she remarked bitterly, and having been rigidly, boringly sober for months I could see her point only too clearly. If I was going to be breast-feeding then responsible for the care of a small child I reckoned it would be at least another two years before I could get even mildly tipsy, but planning a riotous drunken spree was not what I was supposed to be doing when I was about to become a mother. Strangely, I couldn't help looking forward to getting into the sort of state that was so unattractive when I witnessed it in others. It was quite some time before I managed it, which is when I realised the full horror of the combination of children and hangovers.

67. I'M WIDE AWAKE AND I'M WORRIED

Wouldn't it be an excellent idea to be able to sleep for 24 hours solid and then stay up for three days? Why can you catch up on lost sleep but not save up lots of hours so you don't get tired? I began thinking about all those broken nights that people helpfully kept reminding me were coming up soon and wishing I could catch up on the sleep before I lost it. I'd jump into bed (well, heave myself into bed) at 10pm sharp and *will* myself into a deep slumber, even when I wasn't particularly tired, just because I still could. It didn't work. Even if I had slept deeply for a full 12 hours, another 12 hours later and I would be yawning again, not using the four hours I'd gained to knit bootees or re-tile the bathroom.

Even before the baby was born, sleep became a matter of some anxiety. It's one of those irritating dilemmas of life that drifting into a deep refreshing sleep is exactly what you *can't* do when you're in a state of panic about not getting enough sleep.

BIRTH STOOLS

It's not just the baby that pops out, you know. Along with a fine crop of haemorrhoids you can expect some other bodily fluids to make their escape from one or other of your orifices. And not just fluids. I was horrified to learn that there was a distinct possibility that I would crap myself during labour.

I was reassured that midwives are quite used to this and have a special little scoop to whip the offending matter away before anybody notices. I wasn't having any of this, however, and spent the last couple of weeks of my pregnancy constantly emptying my bowels so there couldn't possibly be anything in there to appear when I was least expecting it. This was a little time-consuming and not always productive, but I was determined that my baby would greet the world by itself, and not with any extra little presents to accompany it. I fervently wished nobody had told me about this particular aspect of the miracle of birth.

69. OLD MIDWIVES' TALE

The friend who gleefully told me about the involuntary bowel movements knew what she was talking about because she also happened to be a midwife. So she spent hours regaling me with stories of various indignities and embarrassments that are visited upon women in labour. I swear she enjoyed doing it as well.

Despite her reassurances that there is absolutely nothing that would surprise a midwife, I hoped desperately that I wouldn't be like the woman who farted so much that the staff had to open a window, or the very nice lady who came out with a stream of such startling obscenities that even the baby was red-faced. The pain didn't bother me at all – they have stuff for that – but the prospect of looking like an idiot during the most important process of my life since my own birth I found deeply depressing. I only cheered up when my friend's husband told me that when she was in labour she actually *bit* her own midwife. Fancy her not including that in her catalogue of amusing labour capers.

45. SORRY, DO I KNOW YOU?

When you're padding about behind a large protuberance it's kind of obvious that you've got a baby in there. It's what people first think of when they set eyes on you, just as you know what happens when you are introduced to someone with colossal face furniture. Suddenly your conversation is peppered with anecdotes about the Duke of Wellington, Barry Manilow and Jimmy Durante. You can't help it, and it's the same for anyone faced with a pregnant woman. Even so, that's no excuse for some people's behaviour. You could call it a friendly interest in your condition, if you're feeling magnanimous; if you're feeling a bit peevish you could call it breathtaking nosiness.

I've never had anybody in a supermarket queue comment on the colour of my hair or wonder out loud how I got the graze on my knee (long pre-pregnancy story involving wine at lunchtime and rollerblades) and I would be rather taken aback if it ever happened. Being pregnant, however, makes you public property and you are obliged to answer a lot of personal questions from complete strangers. And you *are* obliged to answer. Pregnant women are ambassadors for their sex and are not allowed to be rude, aggressive or sarcastic when faced with prying questions.

I absolutely hated it, but however misplaced I might have thought it was, I had to admit that most of the time it *was* merely a friendly interest and I was just being boorish. But some people really do go too far. I'm not the only woman to have been absolutely flabbergasted when a complete stranger wanted to put their hand on my frontal swelling. There's a difference between a friendly interest and physical assault, and there's a difference between being regarded as public property and a laboratory animal. I couldn't believe it until I found out that it had happened to other women as well, and they were just as horrified as I was. Honestly, it's bad enough being prodded and poked by qualified doctors without mad old women starting on you.

46. WINNIE THE BLOODY POOH

I don't blame A A Milne, but Walt Disney has a lot to answer for. A couple of trips to Mothercare and I could feel the badly drawn bear's eyes following me round the room. Cutesy and spooky at the same time, that bloody bear gave me the horrors. Still does, actually.

47.   WILD MISCALCULATIONS

Numeracy (or 'doing sums' as we used to call it) has never been my strong point. A pregnancy lasts nine months, which is a small enough number for me to cope with. I thought of myself as roughly three months, five months or eight months pregnant, give or take. Obviously that's not accurate enough for the professionals, who insist on bringing weeks into the equation. 'At 26 weeks your baby will be deciding on its A level subjects and blowing raspberries . . .' Hang on, how long is 26 weeks? I always had to divide by four in order to give myself a better idea of exactly how pregnant I would be after 26 weeks. Six-and-a-half months makes much more sense to me, and I never got the hang of dealing with larger numbers. 'Not very big at all', 'quite big' or 'bloody enormous' was as accurate as I got in terms of calculating my gestation period. Besides which, nine months sounds shorter than 42 weeks. In fact, it is shorter, so my system is much better at ignoring the fact that you are going to be pregnant for *absolutely ages*.

48. JUST TELL ME TO PUT A SOCK IN IT

Naturally I had big ideas for my baby. My mistake was to talk about them. With a foolish bravado bordering on insanity I informed friends with children that I was going to continue working while dandling the baby on my knee; I was going to use ecologically-friendly washable nappies (where I thought I was going to dry them in a first-floor flat without a tumble drier I really can't imagine); I'd make sure the baby slept well; we would only allow educational toys (oh, please); straight after labour I would start exercising to get my body back to normal; I would never lose my temper with my child.

The list of inane and impractical ideas I was happy to spout was endless, but nobody said a word. Friends dealing with sleepless babies, wobbly tummies, nappy buckets and fractious children just let me prattle on, allowing me my rose-tinted dreams while I still had the chance. I suppose it is considered a kindness to pregnant women to let them down gently, but really I wish somebody had pointed out what rubbish I was talking. The arrogance of talking to people who already had children about how I was going to bring up my own child (not like they did, was the unspoken assertion) makes me cringe when I think about it now, but there must be something about being pregnant that warps your brain somehow. Actually, everything about being pregnant seems to warp your brain somehow, so pregnant women should be very careful about expressing any opinions. You never know when people are whispering behind their hands 'Don't worry about her, it's just the hormones talking.'

49. THERE IS LIFE OUTSIDE MOTHERCARE

I couldn't entirely give up expressing opinions, of course. I may have been pregnant, but the rest of the world outside my womb was progressing as normal and I didn't stop taking an interest. The trouble was that the most interesting thing about me was my condition, so I had to give a run-down (run down being the operative words) on my state of health and state of girth before I could start talking about the state of the nation. I might have been bristling with fascinating insights into world politics or the latest Martin Amis but my blood pressure and sleep patterns had to be got out of the way first.

It was kind of people to ask, of course, but I wasn't just pregnant; I was a wise and witty woman as well. Wasn't I? Had I turned into a mere vessel, a walking carrycot for something that wasn't even going to be able to speak, let alone have a conversation, but would be of more interest than its packaging? Naturally, having got myself into a state of high dudgeon because people weren't taking me seriously enough as a person, I would be equally irritated if they failed to ask about me and the baby. 'Yes, well, never mind about the fall of the government for *just* one second. What about *me*? Ask about *me*. I am *pregnant*, don't forget!' I know you are allowed a few mood swings, but my illogicality reached new heights as my waist reached new widths.

70. IT'S DEFINITELY A GIRL OR A BOY

Just as there are people who claim to be able to spot a three days pregnant woman at 20 paces, there are also plenty more who can tell the sex of your baby by the shape of your bum. ('No, really, it was always like that, I don't think it means I'm carrying triplets.') Low-slung bumps contain girl babies; ones you can barely see over the top of are bound to produce a boy. Or so people will have you believe.

Even if you actually know whether you are having a boy or a girl, you will be bombarded with barmy theories about belly shapes, length and severity of morning sickness or heartburn, male versus female sleep patterns and kicking habits, strange skin pigmentations and whether there was a full moon when you conceived. Given that everybody has a 50-50 chance of being right, people obviously feel confident enough to enlarge on their opinions, no matter how much you might protest: 'Yes, well, just because you were sicker with John than with Mary it doesn't actually mean anything about *my* pregnancy, does it?'

People (well, mostly women) who have done it before you know much more than you do about your own body and will insist on projecting their own experiences on to you. You can draw them diagrams but they still have that 'Ah, well, you're new to this and as an old hand at it I obviously have the right to patronise you' attitude. There's absolutely no point in arguing. Just nod and smile as your eyes glaze over, and when you have a daughter when you have been informed without any shadow of a doubt that you were expecting a son, just see how many people remember what they said to you when you were still pregnant. Not many.

71.   I'M LOSING HANDS DOWN

Have you ever had the problem of not knowing what to do with your hands? Get pregnant – problem solved. The simple act of standing up will cause them to gravitate immediately to the small of your back in the classic pregnancy pose.

Everything about this stance says weariness, aches, pains and discomfort. It's not pretty, it's not elegant and it makes you feel tired just to look at it, let alone do it. It also has the advantage of making your belly stick out even further, just in case people hadn't noticed it before.

When I realised I was doing it again and tried to adopt a more dynamic posture, my hands, of their own accord, fluttered gently and came to rest on the top of my stomach. Which looked even worse, of course. I might as well have carried around a dirty great neon arrow. At least I would have had something to do with my hands.

72. WELL, IF I HAD HER MONEY . . .

I never really cared much if celebrities started breeding or not. There always seemed to be plenty of them around so I guessed they weren't about to become extinct, but how they propagated their species wasn't really of much interest to me. But a rash of glamorous pregnancies coinciding with my own decidedly unglamorous one caused me to suspect they were doing it on purpose just to annoy me.

Not only were they better looking than me in the first place, with nicer clothes, more interesting things to do and no obvious signs of nausea in public, they were getting themselves photographed coming out of restaurants and going to premieres while evidently pregnant. If just one of them had been snapped falling down drunk outside a nightclub with mascara running down her face, or sprinting for the loo with an elegantly manicured hand clapped over her mouth, I might have felt less grumpy. Even telling myself that they, too, all had mucous plugs was no consolation. No, it was always 'The lovely Trudi Wastrell, star of the smash hit West End show

Oops, there go my knickers and seen recently on TV's *I'm a celebrity, what's the point of me?* snapped here looking radiant just minutes before the birth in London's prestigious Port Said Clinic by Caesarian section of her daughter Gonorrhea.'

These women will insist on swanning about in beautiful, flattering clothes, with all their own teeth and hair and glowing skin, and looking really bloody happy about it. Well, who wouldn't look happy if they had an army of professionals following them round to rearrange their eyebrows and remove specks from their lapels? I might look a bit more shevelled if I had a personal designer, fitness trainer and astrologer pandering to my every whim.

The fact that my idea of a lifestyle coach is getting National Express because it's cheaper than the train means that seeing photos of groomed and gorgeous women in advanced stages of pregnancy was guaranteed to get my goat. And I knew it wasn't going to get any better because there were no prizes for guessing who would bo the first to fit back into a slinky size 10 evening gown after the birth. Not me. I considered writing to a few of them and asking for their cast-off maternity clothes because they would no doubt fit me until the child started school, but that felt like begging, and I shouldn't really be encouraging these people. I've no real objection to glamorous celebrities getting pregnant if they feel they must, but do they have to rub our noses in it?

73. STAIRWAY TO HELL

On some days you might as well have asked me to climb Everest as to just nip up the stairs. The intense weariness and immediate droop of my shoulders when I realised I'd just staggered down five steps and the thing I wanted was at the top of them was sometimes too much to bear.

Stairs. Such ordinary things that I'd never even thought about them before, but molehills really do become mountains when you are carrying so much extra ballast. I want ground floors, rolling plains, everything on the same level. Death to hills, I say, and slight inclines should be attacked with sledgehammers and made to be flat. Just don't expect me to do it. Not in my condition.

74.   HA! FOOLED YOU!

Braxton Hicks. A stupid name for a stupid thing. I was warned that I could get these from about 28 weeks (six and a bit months in old money), but that they wouldn't be regular. On the contrary, they annoyed me quite regularly, not least when they went under their other name: false contractions. They're not false at all, they are very real – I certainly wasn't imagining them. The only difference between them and the proper thing is that they don't mean you are going in to labour.

So what's the point of them? Couldn't we quite easily do without them, so that when we feel contractions we can say to ourselves 'Hello, Thunderbirds are go' not 'Hello, this is probably nothing but I'd better get the stopwatch out anyway, just in case.' Oh no, it's just another of those pointless little quirks of pregnancy, thrown into the boiling pot of weird symptoms. I say get rid of them, they serve no useful purpose, but nobody seems to be listening to me.

75. IF IT WALKS LIKE A DUCK IT MUST BE A PREGNANT WOMAN

A forceful stride or an elegant glide – anything but that awful rolling waddle I had to adopt in order to get from A to B. But at least a duck can put on a turn of speed if needs be – the idea of doing anything at a brisk pace became increasingly remote as my body became more leaden.

Running for a bus had been about the most athletic thing I had done in years, but I began to long for wide open spaces through which to canter with the wind in my hair. I imagined that once this was all over I would take as much pleasure in taking a running jump as I did when I was about seven. Even a normal walking pace would be nice. In the meantime, anybody who requested that I speed up a little could take a running jump right there and then. Everybody had to come down to my level and slow down – irritating for both them and me as we made our stately way down the high street, watching helplessly as snails and Zimmer frames whizzed past and disappeared into the distance.

76. TO SLEEP, PERCHANCE TO PUNCH THE PILLOW AND WRESTLE THE DUVET

What am I supposed to do with this dirty great protuberance when I'm in bed? Not a line from a seaside postcard but a genuine query from someone who has tried every position possible short of standing on her head in order to try to get comfortable for sleep. If I lay on my back I would either be woken by cramps in my legs or by my partner shaking me awake with spurious complaints about snoring. Our experimenting in bed was now limited to trying out how many pillows it would take to prop up various parts of my body to achieve some limited degree of comfort.

And I don't think I'm alone in *not* lying stock still in the arms of Morpheus. That's not sleep, it's either unconsciousness or death – I like to move about a bit when I'm asleep. But if I had a pillow under my thighs, when I turned over it could get tangled round my knees (I don't know how a pillow gets tangled, but it did), creep silently up under the duvet and join forces with the others in an attempt to suffocate me, or just fall off the bed entirely.

It wasn't that I was tossing and turning – that would have necessitated a certain amount of physical agility – it was more a question of heaving and lumbering my way around the sheets. In seafaring terms, I had turned from a nippy little skiff into a huge ocean liner. And if my partner thought he had escaped temporarily from my fidgety little night-time scamperings, he was still disturbed by the groans and sighs that accompanied my massive manoeuvres, and by the fact that if I did manage to heave my body over to one side, its massive bulk took three-quarters of the duvet with it as well. Not only was I uncomfortable, I was unpopular as well. Not a nice position to be in – as if I would ever again know what a nice position was.

77.   GETTING A BIT EXERCISED

I had drilled into me the importance of keeping myself trim during pregnancy (are you having a laugh or what?). Aerobics were out, thank God, but there was flexing and stretching and tailor sitting and squatting to be done. Not that I was to risk wearing myself out at all. There wasn't much danger of that, as just looking at the exercise plan immediately brought on a feeling of intense weariness. I could just about manage to flap my wrists and ankles a bit before flicking through the advice manuals, trying in vain to find something that said 'If, during the later stages of pregnancy, you just feel like lying around on the sofa eating cream cakes then that's fine – go for it'. I never found anything of the sort, just lots of pictures of women with straight backs and toned thighs, none of whom would recognise a cream cake if it bit them on the bum. Assuming that a cream cake could actually find a bum that tiny.

78.   İT'S WASTED ON ME

For the first time in my life I was undeniably, gloriously, luxuriantly, largely womanly. (In other words, you wouldn't catch a bloke getting pregnant.) Never before had I enjoyed full frontage. My chest, previously a rather ordinary affair, had become a bosom. Two of them, in fact, separated by what could only be described as a cleavage. A real one – not a toe one, not a bum one – a breast one.

The new-found possibilities were endless. The words 'plunging neckline', 'voluptuous' and 'Jayne Mansfield', previously only read in books (well, rather trashy magazines, actually) were now a part of my new life. This was great! Well, it would have been great, if the generous mammary area hadn't been resting on an even more generous tummy area. Just try putting your shoulders back and thrusting foward your twin peaks when you are heavily pregnant. It was possible, I found, for my globes of loveliness to be overshadowed by something beneath them.

So any thoughts of presenting myself to the world as an overstuffed sofa instead of the usual ironing board were somewhat scuppered by the fact that the stuffing was everywhere, not just in the upper storeys. Plus the fact that my image as a beauteous sex goddess was undoubtedly marred by the fact that sex goddesses very rarely fascinate their adoring audiences by lumbering off to the toilet every 10 minutes in between complaining about varicose veins and heartburn.

'Couldn't I keep the chest and lose the stomach accompaniment?' I wheedled to Mother Nature, who gave a cruel laugh and answered viciously: 'Who do you think you are? A celebrity or something? The stomach stays.' For quite some time after the birth of the baby, as I found out.

79.   STRETCHING A POINT

I once heard a woman admitting with an embarrassed laugh that she rather liked the look of stretchmarks, comparing them to the ripples of retreating waves on a white-sanded beach. I stared hard and tried to imagine my body as a sun-drenched Caribbean resort. It was about as successful as the time I stared hard at the lawn and tried to convince myself that dandelions are really rather attractive flowers. But even dandelions are easier to get rid of than stretchmarks.

80. ATTACK OF THE 60FT WOMAN

'God, look at that elephant in a tent. Oh, it's me' was a thought that often crossed my mind if I accidentally looked into a shop window or passed a mirror large enough to accommodate my bulk. If I had to look in a mirror I would approach it with caution, psyching myself up for a shock of unrecognition every time.

It was the unexpected glimpses that always caught me by surprise, which were even worse than the unfamiliar reflection in a familiar mirror. I could have sworn I looked halfway decent when I left the house, but that humongous woman in the plate glass window says different. Screams it, in fact. And the shocked expression on her face doesn't help, either.

There are such things as mirrors that lie, aren't there? Please tell me that there is something in glass that increases the size of whatever it reflects. In fact, I'm sure of it and if I were clever enough I could probably prove it with a series of mathematical calculations. Or would that just be smoke and mirrors?

81. JUST LOOK AT THE STATE OF MY DRAWERS

I'm really going to be big about this (seeing as how I'm big about everything else). I refuse to do the obvious thing and I am not going to be a slave to my hormones. Oh, yes you are. Even household sluts get the nesting instinct, apparently. Cupboards that have looked like jumble sales for years are suddenly turned out and tidied. Mr Sheen will be begging you for some respite when your previously unknown cleaning genes take over.

It's nice, in a way, to have a well-ordered knicker drawer for the first time ever, and folding muslin squares is a pleasant, mumsy-type thing to do. The nesting instinct is all very well, but what happened to the instinct for delegation? Shouldn't I be lying on the sofa barking instructions to menials, not putting CDs in alphabetical order and polishing the cat? My consolation was that it's only a passing phase and that shortly after the birth of the baby the place was bound to return to its normal condition of complete tip. I couldn't let the child get the impression that I was always going to be washing houseplants and ironing shoelaces. No, no, that would never do.

82. HEAVE-HO AND AWAY WE GO - AGAIN

Hello! It's my old friend nausea back to greet me. Only this time it's different. The vomit hasn't changed much, admittedly – the queasiness, sweating and eye-watering taste of bile is all too, too familiar. But here's a new twist to an old tale: now it can happen at any time at all. Morning, afternoon, evening – it's all the same to the barf fairy. Only, it's not a barf fairy causing me to execute the technicolour yawn at a moment's notice, is it? It's a dirty great baby taking up room inside me that was already full, as far as I know – I mean, I'm damn sure I wasn't hollow before I got pregnant.

So where's the baby going to fit? Well, it's not, obviously. Something's got to give, and what gives is your internal organs. With my stomach squeezed into the space of a matchbox to make way for knees, elbows and an entire head, it was no wonder I felt sick. It's not normal to have your insides compacted like a bunch of car wrecks, is it? Oh, sorry, I forgot. When you are pregnant, 'normal' is just a whole load of bonkers stuff. Oh well, I didn't feel much like eating, anyway.

83. COULD YOU PICK THAT UP FOR ME?

Had somebody secretly smeared my hands with butter when I wasn't looking? Did I always drop things with such wearisome regularity, or did it only happen when I was incapable of picking them up again? 'Slippery digits' had never come up in the endless list of pregnancy symptoms, but then it would hardly be worth telling a pregnant woman about all the things that were going to happen to her body. The kid would be at university by the time you got to the end of it.

On the other hand, this inability to hold anything with a firm grasp could just come under the general heading of sod's law. Naturally, if you can't bend down without a complicated system of ropes and pulleys, everything you have in your hands is going to leap out and either smash to smithereens or lie mockingly on the floor, just out of reach. Butter side down, usually.

Most of the time this was just irritating, as another book or cup tumbled from my nerveless fingers, but also faintly disturbing, as I considered that soon I would be carrying something a little more valuable, which couldn't be kicked under the carpet if dropped. Was the baby aware of all these bangs and crashes, and getting suspicious of its mother's competence? Suppose it refused to leave the security of the womb until I had been passed by the Health and Safety Executive? So that was something else to worry about. Oh good.

84. BE PREPARED

'Pack your hospital bag in plenty of time' I was advised, which is actually pretty good advice. You don't want to be flailing around trying to find your bedsocks when amniotic fluid is splashing round your ankles. But what would I really need? Mascara, for example. Is that an essential item? I imagined that after having given birth to a baby I would be more in need of full slap than at any other time in my life, but regretfully decided that I probably wouldn't have a lot of time for applying lipgloss and would have to rely on my natural glow. People wouldn't be looking at me, anyway, but homing in on the baby, so might not notice if I looked a little haggard.

But even if they weren't scrutinising my open pores, visitors and health professionals couldn't help but notice the sorry state of my nightwear. I can scrub up pretty well when in public, but tend to assume that people aren't going to be assessing my wardrobe while I'm snoring and dribbling (apart from those few times on the late-night train home, of course, but that hadn't happened for a *very* long time). So I'd wear any old thing in bed, if anything at all. The National Health Service frowns on nudity unless they've requested it themselves, but with a new baby on the way, was this really the time to invest money in (squander money on) attractive yet practical bedwear? The vain fashion-hag said yes; the prudent mother-to-be said no.

So I dutifully collected the essential items for a short hospital stay, and I must say I have never before packed more dispiriting luggage. If I were going away for a weekend I would throw in favourite clothes and underwear, dinky little travel-sized cleansers and cosmetics and perhaps some perfume and jewellery. My hospital bag contained among other things bulky sanitary towels, ghastly disposable knickers (they were so horrid I nearly disposed of them before they were used), a strictly efficient-looking maternity bra and a rather threadbare striped nightshirt affair that made me look like an aged Wee Willie Winkie. This was not going to be my most glamorous city break. (Incidentally, you know what I forgot? Nappies. I had to buy some from the hospital shop, even though I had stacks at home. They didn't sell mascara. I checked.)

85. BUT YOU CAN'T

Apart from the nappies, I thought I was pretty well prepared for my little hospital sojourn. I'd done all the right things and was settled in for the home straight. We had all the right equipment, clothes, a room waiting – all we needed now was a baby. Easy peasy. But it doesn't matter if you've planned the pregnancy and birth like a military operation; people won't stop telling you that you can't possibly prepare yourself for the birth of a baby. They seem to take real pleasure in assuring you that you will be a sleep-deprived quivering jelly within a week, and there's absolutely nothing you can do about it. I remember threatening to scream louder than any hungry baby if I heard again the phrase 'Of course, you won't know what's hit you until it happens.'

86. HAVE YOU DONE ENOUGH PREPARATION?

Fair enough. If there's nothing I can do about it, there's no point in brooding on this thing that's going to hit me. I shall play it by ear and not be surprised by anything that happens – seeing as everybody keeps telling me that preparation is pointless. Having agreed wearily with smug parents that no, I had no idea what it was going to be like, I then encountered the opposite camp of concerned busybodies who insisted on quizzing me on my psychological readiness for my impending motherhood.

Asking a woman in the final stages of pregnancy whether she has really thought this through is inane, but it didn't stop people doing it. What could I say? I've thought of precious little else for the last nine months, actually, but that lot over there keep telling me there's no point because you can't imagine what having a baby is like until you've got one. Now you're telling me I ought to be doing more mental preparation for something I have no experience of. I'm tired and confused so why don't you all just shut up and leave me alone? I've got a baby to have.

87.   HIGH ANXIETY

Naturally, even though I tried to ignore all this unwanted advice, it still wormed its nagging little way into my brain. How well prepared was I really? What had I learnt in those antenatal classes? Whatever it was I'd forgotten it all, and experienced the same feeling of rising panic as when an exam approaches for which you know you haven't done enough revision.

What were the stages of labour? How do you time contractions? How do you know when it's time to go to hospital? How are you supposed to breathe? When do you push? When don't you push? What's my name? Where am I? I was in no fit state to absorb important information, and stared helplessly and hopelessly at instruction manuals on what to do when you think you are going into labour, desperately trying to remember the difference between a long breath out and a short breath in, a push and a pull until I barely knew which way was up.

I took to writing myself little notes, but gave up on that as well in the end, and just made a huge placard that said DON'T PANIC! I can't say it helped much, and it did tend to make visitors a little twitchy when they saw it propped up on the mantelpiece. Besides which, constantly catching sight of a large exhortation *not* to panic simply reminded me to do the exact opposite. I panicked.

88.   WHAT WAS GOD THINKING ABOUT?

Despite all evidence to the contrary (a fully populated world, women with more than one child), as due date approached I looked at all the diagrams, even photos, and decided that what was about to happen to me was not physically possible. I spent fruitless hours thinking about skinny little snakes that dislocate their jaws in order to swallow herds of wildebeest. Can't say it helped much.

Surely there had to be a more efficient way of ensuring the survival of the human race? There is something so distressingly medieval about the whole business. Has evolution stopped? Kangaroos have the right idea. They give birth to something about the size of a peanut which then has to crawl unaided into its mother's pouch where it grows outside her body, giving her no trouble at all – not making her sick, keeping her awake at night or giving her stretchmarks. When you find yourself wishing to be a kangaroo instead of a human being you know you've been pregnant for too long. Anyway, the answer I got to the question 'Would you still fancy me if I was a marsupial?' wasn't terribly encouraging.

89.   TIME FLIES WHEN YOU'RE HAVING FUN

When I wasn't lumbering around complaining bitterly about the interminable length of the human pregnancy, I was frantically adding up the days and praying for a little more time. No, no, I'm really not ready yet! I didn't mean all that stuff about how much bloody longer is this going to take. I really don't mind being this size at all. It's fine. I could do it for another month at least. Why, I've never read *War and Peace* or watched the whole of the *Red Dwarf* series. Surely another couple of weeks couldn't hurt – I promise I will never grumble about swollen ankles again. Given that I'm the size of an elephant anyway, couldn't I have the elephant's gestation period?

Swinging wildly between impatience to get it all over with and a deep anxiety about what was going to happen next wasn't the best way to prepare myself for becoming a mother but it was the only way I knew.

90. WE'RE IN THIS TOGETHER, DEAR

Naturally, when the time came I could rely on the help and support of the baby's father. Couldn't I? Entirely unsympathetic to his anxieties about impending childbirth, I warned him that he was welcome to stick around if he wanted to, but he should be prepared for me to swear, get extremely stroppy and hurl abuse. (In the event, I did hurl, but it wasn't abuse, just good old-fashioned vomit – all over his clean shirt.)

Had I not been so self-absorbed I might have noticed that he too was getting a little green around the gills at the thought of the blood, sweat and tears we were about to enjoy together. Selfishly, I thought that as it was me who was going to be doing the dirty work, he would just have to put up with it. I think my instructions to him were along the lines of 'Don't run out of petrol, don't faint, don't get in the way, don't try to be useful and for God's sake stay at the head end.'

91.　Oh, shut up you idiot

Whenever I heard some poncy pundit burbling pompously something like 'Well, you're either in or out of the EU. I mean, you can't be a "little bit pregnant". Fnargh, fnargh!' I would spit viciously 'Au contraire, mon brave. When you have been pregnant for nine months and you are large, lumbering, tired, bad tempered and every fibre of your being is screaming "Big! Big! Big!" you remember with extreme fondness being "a little bit pregnant".'

92. A WOMB WITH A VIEW

'I have a fully-formed human being living inside my body.' OK, I'd had quite a long time to get used to the idea. Even so, it was a bit of a shock when, flicking idly through a pregnancy manual, I came across – without warning – an artist's impression of what my baby looked like at this stage. A perfectly normal baby – except it had its eyes open.

I'm afraid I snapped the book shut with some violence. I was sure I had all the right maternal instincts, but frankly, that was just creepy. What could it see? What was there to look at? What impressions was it forming of its mother by staring at her insides? Would it be expecting to form a bond with something wet, red and squashy? If so, I had better chuck out that sponge in case I was supplanted in the child's affections by a bath accessory.

I was immensely relieved that babies remember nothing of their babyhood. They don't, do they? The alternative was too horrible to contemplate, so of course I spent several fruitless hours brooding on the possibility that my baby would retain vivid memories of parts of my body that even I had no clear knowledge of. Nice.

93. AN END AND A BEGINNING

'Bet you're looking forward to the end of this now,' people would say comfortingly as soon as I hove into view. Of course, I can't wait to go into labour, experience terrible pain, exhaustion and a series of broken nights stretching far into the future. The thought crossed my mind that after nine months of all the joys of pregnancy what I could really do with was a holiday, not a newborn baby to look after. Shouldn't there be some sort of cooling-off period before you have to re-enter the fray? The more I thought about it, the more certain I was that this pregnancy and birth business really hadn't been thought through properly. I wouldn't be at all surprised if it had been organised by a man. Or, more likely, a committee of men. And if I ever get my hands on them . . .

94.   DON'T ANSWER IT!

Naturally, in the final weeks and days all your friends and family are anxious for news. But instead of waiting, which is a subject I could have given a two-hour lecture on by this stage, they would insist on ringing up to find out. How am I? I'm still bloody pregnant, if that's what you want to know. In my grumpy state I didn't really feel like answering the same old questions with the same old answers ('No, strangely, I haven't been doing much exciting; in fact I haven't been doing much unexciting'), and considered changing the answering machine message to: 'No, nothing's happened yet, but rest assured that when it does you'll be the first to know.' It wasn't as if all these people were expecting to hear 'Oh, yeah, I had the baby three days ago but I haven't got round to telling you yet. How does it feel to be a grandmother/aunt/potential babysitter?' so why couldn't they just wait to be told?

95.　İ DON'T DRİNK, BUT İ FORGET ANYWAY

Being the sort of person who can't get into a taxi to the airport without checking tickets, passport and bags at least five times – before returning home to check that the gas is off and the door locked – the last few days of my pregnancy were spent in an agonising flurry of trying to remember what I had forgotten. Which is a pointless exercise because if you've forgotten something it's because you have forgotten it, or because you never thought of it in the first place.

I drove myself mad trying to imagine situations that hadn't occurred to me before, wondering if I should get in a stock of snake-bite serum and whether it would be a good idea to get all my shoes repaired now, in case I didn't have time later. It wasn't a good recipe for rest and relaxation – and I still managed to forget things anyway.

96. THE DAY

Waking up on the morning of your due date is a very weird experience. Over the months the date has acquired an almost supernatural significance – the day when everything changes. Having worked out the baby's star sign and whether it would be fair of face, full of grace or have far to go, the day that has loomed for so long dawns with a sense of such massive expectancy that you spend it all waiting for something to happen and hypersensitively aware of every twinge, temperature change and heartbeat. Will I become a mother today? When's it going to start? Is there any point in watching the first part of this two-part thriller on the television? You pad about all day in a state of high suspense – and nothing happens.

97. THE DAY AFTER THE DAY

Right, well, we'll start again, shall we? Having spent the previous day at fever pitch of excitement and trepidation you have to reproduce it all again, except the one thing you are *not* doing is reproducing. Will I become a mother today? When's it going to start? Will I be able to catch up on the second part of the thriller I didn't watch yesterday? Then the recalculations begin. Well, if it's not born today then I'd rather it wasn't tomorrow because that's Wednesday – full of woe – but then I'd have to wait even longer and there's always the danger of it being born on the cusp, and the weather forecast isn't very good for Thursday and I don't fancy getting to hospital in a thunderstorm and – oh, *come on* baby, it can't be that comfortable in there! And nothing happens.

98. WHEN WE SAID THE FIFTH OF THE MONTH, WE MIGHT HAVE MEANT THE TWENTY-FIFTH

Yes, I did know that the magical date is subject to a two-week margin of error, but I really can't believe it. I don't want to believe it. I won't believe it. I can't possibly spend another 14 days like the last two – no human being could stand it! But human beings have stood it, as you know perfectly well, having heard all those stories about unfortunate women who apparently suffered 10-month pregnancies. But their babies were born eventually, I told myself, and presumably this one will be too. I'm just not sure when.

Having waited so long I was still pretty certain that two wouldn't turn up at once, but working on the theory that if you light a fag the bus will come, I started on long and complicated sewing projects that would be highly inconvenient to leave at a moment's notice, just to goad the baby into making its entrance (or exit, depending on how you look at it). I didn't care how inconvenient it was, as long as it was *soon*.

99. The perfect time to visit the Taj Mahal

Sewing achieved nothing more than making a mess in the living room. Drastic measures were called for. Ignoring my previous scorn of half-baked theories and old wives' tales, I insisted that we go for a curry. Well it was worth a try! I've often wondered since whether the waiters in Indian restaurants nudge each other in amusement or despair and say 'Look out, here comes another one!' as a heavily pregnant and rather impatient-looking woman lumbers through the door bellowing for vindaloo. If curry does indeed encourage the onset of labour, I wonder if they also ask themselves exactly how quickly it does it, and whether they should have the local maternity hospital on redial or simply add midwifery to their waiting skills. But I've never had the courage to ask.